CW00556568

Acknowledgements

I am indebted to so many people for their help in producing this book that it is impossible to mention them all. Barry Setterfield introduced me to the possibility that there could be major flaws in many of the "scientific" ideas I had believed for many years. I am also grateful that he introduced me to the work of George Dodwell. Mark Kreitzer did me a great service by introducing me to the work of Dr. Walter van der Kamp — and his successor as head of the Tychonian Society, Dr. Gerardus Bouw. Professor Johan Bruinsma, Dr. Henk Jochemsen and Bert Dorenbos gave valuable help with the Appendix. I have also drawn on the work of many scientists who for years have been prepared to accept rebuff by the scientific establishment for questioning the accepted wisdom — Duane Gish, Henry Morris, Robert Gentry, Garry Parker, Andrew Snelling, Herbert Dingle and Thomas Barnes to mention only a few. I am also grateful to Kjell Olsen and Geoff Donnan for their encouragement, and to my wife and children for the way they have accepted that such a project takes much time and attention which might have been spent on them.

VITAL QUESTIONS

by Philip Stott

2nd Edition
©2002 Philip Stott

ISBN 0-9721354-2-1
Publisher:
Reformation Media and Press
13950 - 122nd St.
Fellsmere, Florida 32948-6411 U.S.A.
reformation@direcway.com

Publishing History

Ist Edition : Valamin 1994
2nd Impression: Valamin 1998

Vital Questions

Contents

Preface to the 2nd edition

While this new edition was in preparation, the BBC World Service broadcast a program in a series on the history of Africa. This particular edition was entitled "Origins". It began with a matter of fact narration of the evolution of man from apelike creatures millions of years ago. Towards the end of the program one of the palaeontologists featured let slip the possibility that all was not as watertight as thus far suggested. He pointed out that there was "some evidence" which fits in with the hypothesis that the rest of the program had presented as solidly established fact.

Immediately after this confident account of the origin of man, (with its slightest of slight hints that all might not be 100% established fact), came the news. It was announced that scientists engaged in the human genome project had published the results of its ten year search for the sequence of man's genetic makeup. For years we had been confidently told that man's DNA consisted of vast numbers of genes which control every aspect of our existence - from the colour of our eyes to whether those eyes will need spectacles later in life, from the shape of our feet to the size of the shoes those feet will need, from our mental prowess to our abilities in sport. The researchers announced a great surprise to the eagerly awaiting world. The genome consists of only about thirty thousand recognisable genes, only twice as many as a tiny fruit fly, only three hundred more than a mouse. Far too few to account for the incredible complexity of our anatomy, or the mind-boggling complexity of our thought processes. In the comments after the news a scientist who had been involved with the project pointed out that the small number of genes means that environmental factors must be far more important than had been assumed beforehand.

Scientists seem to have got into a routine. One theory falls in ruins and immediately another is confidently put forward as established fact. With no proof it is now assumed that the environment somehow supplies the vast amount of information which the genome had been expected to give. What about other possibilities? Is there vastly more information in the DNA than the scientists have been able to recognise? Is there a reservoir of information other than DNA in the cells of our body? Is there a supernatural source of information which moulds us to a degree unheard of in today's humanistic culture?

In spite of repeated demonstration that the proud claims of many scientists can be very wrong, the world at large continues to regard their pronouncements with awe. If a scientist says so, it must be true! I believe that this book is as relevant today as when the first edition was published in 1994. New material has been added, other material has been taken out, reflecting to some extent the way scientific fashions have changed. Much of the new information has been taken from the Internet - a source not widely available when the first edition was published. This has the advantage that checking is easy and further research can be undertaken by almost anyone with access to a computer. Internet sources usually have less authority than refereed journals, but with care the Internet is a very valuable resource.

I have had scientists complain that many of the references are to articles in scientific journals more than thirty years old (some, such as references to Darwin's "Origin Of Species", Einstein's papers, Michelson's experiments, etc. are much older than that!) Such criticism is actually acknowledgment that what scientists say today they will not stand by (or will deny) tomorrow. Things accepted by scientists last year may be acknowledged as errors next year. This is a reflection on the virtually "science-free" science of the last hundred years. Real science produces knowledge which stands the test of time. Newtonian mechanics texts of a century ago are similar to those of today. Notation may have changed, new techniques may have been added, but Newtonian mechanics has not changed to any significant degree. What a difference to the situation with Evolution and Cosmology. Many of the statements, speculations and conclusions from texts from only fifty years ago are replaced in modern texts with a significantly different and often contradictory set.

Introduction

In "Some Mysteries of the Universe", written in 1969[1], W.R. Corliss noted that the estimates for the age of the earth and cosmos made by the foremost experts have varied drastically over the years. Not long ago the best estimates suggested an age only a fraction of that currently believed.

Corliss optimistically concluded by saying, "At least today's geological, astronomical, and physical clocks seem to be giving us the same readings; and that is reassuring. The clocks are getting better."

That was in 1969. But Corliss' optimism that science is getting closer to the truth about the universe we live in seems to have been short lived. In 1986, writing in the March-April edition of "DISCOVER", he commented on the terribly complex theories that science is having to propose in order to fit observations into its established world view. He said "As the structures of the Cosmos and the subatomic world become more and more foreign to every-day experience, we have to ask whether such bizarre constructions may not be the consequence of incorrect physical theories, such as Relativity, the Big Bang hypothesis, and so on."

Such a suggestion is not at all popular with the "experts". The suggestion that their cherished theories may be wrong, that they may have been believing, and teaching, ideas that are actually far from the truth, is not at all attractive. History shows that the experts practically never abandon incorrect theories.

---

1 W.R. Corliss, Some Mysteries of the Universe, Adam & Charles Black; London, 1969

Occasionally a great man is prepared to admit that he has been wrong, but as Max Plank remarked "A new scientific truth does not triumph by convincing its opponents and making them see the light, but rather because its opponents eventually die, and a new generation grows up that is familiar with it."[2]

There is abundant evidence that many of the cherished theories of our era are "proper stuff and nonsense". As you consider the information presented in this book remember that the greatest experts have often been wrong. And beware of a trap that many of them fall into. When confronted with powerful evidence that their theories are wrong they often pounce on one or two details of the critique (often minor details with little relevance) which they are convinced they know to be wrong. They then use their "refutation" of some minor details as a licence to close their minds to the main thesis. This book is not primarily concerned with the minor details, it is about the major aspects of our current "knowledge".

---

2 Quoted from Scientific Autobiography, Max Plank

Chapter 1

Do We Know Anything At All?

The wisdom of man has progressed through several stages. The "wise" men, the philosophers of history, long considered that human reason was all that was needed to arrive at knowledge or "truth". But many conclusions reached by pure reason, after being held for centuries perhaps, were found to be simply not true. The problem was that reasoning always had to start with assumptions. The fact that the conclusions were sometimes wrong suggested that the initial assumptions were faulty.

The wise and learned realised that there was much to be said for making measurements and observations and then reasoning about the observations rather than about pure assumptions. The reasons behind this way of thinking are important and interesting, and are touched on in Chapter 8 and the Appendix. It gave rise to the "scientific method". A problem with this idea, though, is that one can only be reasonably sure of the conclusions if every item of data relevant to the problem is available for consideration. This, unfortunately for science, is not usually the case. Huge gaps in available data may have to be filled in by presupposition and assumption. Such assumptions are totally dependent on the world-view, the underlying belief system, of the seeker after knowledge.

The history of science has many remarkable examples of the difficulties which can arise when dubious but attractive ideas become firmly established in scientific thinking. The chemists of three hundred years ago were convinced that fire was caused by something escaping from a burning body. This, of course, is eminently reasonable. A fir cone or a piece of paper, when burned, becomes just a little heap of ash; the form, structure and organisation, as well as much of the volume are gone. Obviously something has been lost. This "something" was given the name "Phlogiston".

Many observations, not only those concerning actual burning, but also such processes as rusting, could be successfully explained by this idea. So many observations were explained by phlogiston that its existence became part of the basic mind-set of scientists. But eventually scientists made observations which did not fit neatly into the phlogiston theory. For example it was found that when a sample was burned and all the products of combustion were weighed, the final weight was greater than the initial weight of the sample. Instead of abandoning the idea that phlogiston was given off, scientists reasoned that phlogiston must have negative mass. To explain other experiments it became necessary to believe that phlogiston had negative volume too, but scientists were so confident of the theory that they were more ready to accept negative mass and negative volume than doubt the existence of phlogiston. Ultimately Lavoisier suggested that combustion was not the loss of phlogiston, but the gaining of oxygen. Nowadays we consider this perfectly obvious, but even great scientists like Joseph Priestley were unable to change their thinking to accept it. Priestley opposed oxidation and supported phlogiston till his dying day.

Illustration 1
For many years scientists believed that when fuel burned it lost phlogiston. It is now believed that it gains oxygen.

This is not an isolated chapter in the history of science, plenty of notable errors have been made in the last hundred years.

Many examples have come from the field of palaeoanthropology, in which scientists examine the remains of humans and apes and then try to fit the remains of unknown creatures into some intermediate group. For about a hundred years palaeontologists have been boldly announcing the discovery of "primitive ancestors of man". The famous American Professor Henry Fairfield Osborne, for example, confidently presented Nebraska Man to the world as a stage in the evolution of man from the apes. This important ape-man was the prime piece of evidence in the famous "Scopes' Trial" in America. The most important outcome of this trial was that it profoundly influenced the decision to accept evolution as the only theory of origins to be taught in American schools. The "fact" of Nebraska man was prime evidence for establishing the "fact" of evolution. Osborne reconstructed Nebraska Man using the same techniques that all palaeontologists use, building up much from little, deducing the whole from part. Nebraska Man was reconstructed from one tooth.

Illustration 2
Nebraska man, like several other ape-men, was reconstructed from one tooth.
It was later found to be a wild pig's tooth.

It is not uncommon to reconstruct an ape-man from one or two teeth.

Osborne reasoned that because the tooth had such a shape, the jaw must have had a particular shape to hold it. Because the jaw had such a form, the skull must have had a specific shape for it to fit onto. To hold such a skull the body must have had such a shape, and so on. Such reasoning produced not only Nebraska Man, but also his tools, his wife, her cooking utensils and the hut they lived in. Nebraska Man took his place on the "family tree of Man" with the impressive scientific name "Hesperopithecus", and there he remained until an identical tooth was found in the company of a considerable part of its original owner. It was rather embarrassing to note that the more complete remains were those of a wild pig! And this is not an isolated example. Ramapithecus was reconstructed from speculation concerning a tooth missing from a bit of jawbone. After many years of tremendous publicity as one of man's early ancestors Ramapithecus had to be abandoned as yet another mistake ... although the missing tooth was never found, the bit of jawbone was eventually recognised as that of a gibbon. Another well-known "ape man" was reconstructed from what its reconstructors described as a perfect ape-man skull-cap. It was later identified as an elephant's knee cap. Yet another "ancestor of man" was reconstructed from what was believed to be part of an ape-man's collar-bone. It was later found to be part of a dolphin's rib. Even today we hear of palaeontologists presenting reconstructions of "man's early ancestors" from scraps of bone and a few teeth. [1]

Obviously it is not the evidence provided by observation and experiment which is the cause of these tremendous errors, it is the mind-set of the scientists interpreting the evidence in terms of their beliefs and theories. The idea that man must have evolved from some ape-like creature has become so deeply ingrained in the world-view of palaeontology that the existence of intermediate "ape-men" was not doubted. There was complete confidence that remains must be in existence, simply waiting to be discovered. It became easy to fall victim to the delusion that such remains had, at last, been found.

---

1 In July 2002 the respected journal Nature carried an article on a new "important" discovery from Chad based on part of a cranium and two fragments of jawbone. Palaeontologists noted that they would have to re-evaluate their theories of human evolution because of this find. Michael Behe, a well known professor of biochemistry made a very pertinent comment ..."If the discovery of one new set of bones makes palaeontologists re-evaluate what they knew, they really didn't know all that much."

The world view, the essential idea which guides scientists in their thinking is nowadays popularly called the "paradigm". The prevailing paradigm today is based on secular humanism. It holds that life is a purely natural phenomenon which came about through biological evolution. It holds that the earth, the planets, the stars and everything in the universe are purely natural phenomena which came about by natural processes of material evolution. Almost all scientists nowadays interpret their data in terms of this paradigm.

Until the middle of the 19th century almost all scientists held to a completely different paradigm, the paradigm of divine creation. For most scientists the God of the Bible had created the universe and everything in it much as we see it today; they interpreted their observations in the light of this world-view. Their interpretation of observations of the earth, the universe and life were completely different even though the earth, the universe and the creatures were the same.

Science is not the infallible source of true knowledge that many have been led to believe. It relies heavily on the views of the scientists themselves. Then is there any way of knowing something for sure? One way might be to accept "self-evident truths". Descartes convinced himself that "I think, therefore I am" is a self-evident truth on which he could build absolutely certain knowledge.

But self-evident truths are not immune to philosophical dissection. Think for example of the self-evident truth that a watch needs a designer. It is hard to imagine anyone honestly doubting that a watch could come into existence without having been deliberately designed by a creative intelligence — a designer. However, how does one answer a philosopher who asks "But how do you know it was designed? How do you know it was not just formed naturally like a crystal in a bed of rock?"

It would obviously not suffice to say, "I have never found any beds of rock with watches embedded in them" — our philosopher can retort, "But you have not examined every bed of rock in the universe, so how can you be sure that they do not come from beds you have not visited?"

The next idea might be to take the sceptical philosopher to a watch-making factory. You show him the complex machinery manufacturing the parts according to a drawing which clearly represents the ideas of a designer. But this is still inadequate. Our sceptic can respond, "Ah, yes, but there are also factories with complex machines which manufacture diamonds, and there are drawings showing the form of the diamonds that those machines are making. But diamonds occur naturally as crystals in rock, the artificial diamond making machinery is simply copying a naturally occurring object which does not require a designer. How do you know that at this factory the blueprints are not simply drawings of a naturally occurring watch?"

Perhaps the next step might be to take the philosopher to meet the designer, and have him explain that he did not copy a naturally occurring accident, but really did design it himself. "But how do you know that he is telling the truth? He might be deliberately telling lies in order to make money from his ill-gotten copyright, or he might have deluded himself and is lying unintentionally."

Perhaps it might seem that this is a rather silly example. For all his perversity, anyone with the intelligence to ask such searching questions realises that a watch requires a designer, even though he can challenge every scrap of evidence for the truth of that fact. But it is actually not a silly example at all. The human eye is a vastly more complex piece of machinery than a watch, and obviously also required a designer. Charles Darwin, in his famous book The Origin Of Species said:- "To suppose that the eye with all its inimitable contrivances for adjusting the focus to different distances, for admitting different amounts of light, and for the correction of spherical and chromatic aberration, could have been formed by natural selection, seems, I freely confess, absurd in the highest degree." And yet that is exactly what is required for belief in the theory of evolution. In the same way that one can argue for a naturally occurring watch, one can argue for a naturally occurring eye. Darwin recognised the impossibility of that as a self-evident truth, and yet it is still possible to make a case for its possibility, a case so convincing that many accept it.

We cannot rely on self-evident truths.

Another solution to the problem of knowledge has become popular today:- a return to the wisdom of the most ancient philosophies and religions of the world. The movement advocating this step is somewhat incongruously called the "New Age Movement". Many intellectuals, realising the inadequacy of science and philosophy to answer their deepest needs, are turning to it. They rely on four sources for true knowledge.

The first source is the elite group who has "made it" and reached the goal to which the remainder is heading: spiritual unity with the cosmos ... effectively godhood. Many members of the movement regard this knowledge with great esteem and are prepared to pay considerable sums to attend seminars and instruction sessions given by these masters. Non-members have expressed doubts though. There seems to be an element of getting rich quickly which is reminiscent of certain other rather dubious religious movements.

The second source of knowledge is in the pronouncements of spirits speaking through mediums; it has become fashionable to use the word "channel" rather than "medium". It is certainly true that throughout history there have been examples of spiritualists able to report facts which could later be verified to be true. But a question has been repeatedly raised. How does one know that this is not just to arouse confidence, so that when other information, which cannot be checked, is given, it will also be believed, whether true or not. The New Agers often consider the spirits to be angels, so their honesty is not to be doubted. Throughout history, however, there are those who have been convinced that the spirits conjured up by mediums are demons, and therefore not to be trusted at all!

The third source of knowledge is somewhat similar. One meditates, practices yoga, chants a mantra or follows some similar regime until one makes contact with a "spirit guide", who is able to impart knowledge. Exactly the same question arises concerning the nature of these spirit guides. New Agers report them as being beautiful, friendly, loving, helpful. But then, throughout history it has been held that Satan appears as an angel of light. There are certainly some who doubt the benevolent nature and the reliability of spirit guides!

The fourth source of knowledge is simply the certainty within oneself that something is so. New Agers argue that when they have reached a "state of consciousness in harmony with the universe" they instinctively know the truth. But the bizarre pronouncements of some of those supposedly having attained this state of consciousness do not always inspire confidence that this is so. There seems to remain a strong element of doubt, especially among non-New Agers, that personal conviction is not actually a guarantee of truth. It looks as if we cannot rely on the knowledge gained by the methods and beliefs of the occult religions of the ancient East, even if given a new name.

Then is there any sure method of knowing real truth? In all the methods we have seen, knowledge is, in the final analysis, strongly influenced by faith. The New Ager's knowledge is obviously faith, but that of the scientist (although many scientists hate to admit it!) is also a matter of faith; it depends on how his world view allows him to interpret his data. The knowledge — or rejection of knowledge — of the philosopher, in the same way depends on what he is prepared to accept as reasonable.

If we are prepared to accept this essential necessity of faith in coming to any real knowledge then it would be logical to consider Divine revelation as another source of knowledge. Here we run into the difficulty that there are several documents purporting to be divine revelation, some so contradictory to the others as to be clearly mutually exclusive. There is the Bible of the Christians, the Koran of the Moslems, the Tapitaka of the Buddhists, etc. Is there anything to choose between them? Is there any way of deciding which, if any, has a valuable contribution to make to knowledge and truth. Most observers would admit that one, the Bible, stands out in several ways. One of these is the astounding fierceness and persistence of the opposition which it has faced; opposition on a scale unknown to any of the others. Leaders of the Roman empire attempted to destroy every copy. For centuries the Church of Rome made it a crime, punishable by death, for a layman to own one. Secular humanist scientists of the last two centuries have attacked it, ridiculed it and gone to great lengths to disprove it. Philosophers have directed much of their time and effort towards discrediting it. The communist regime of the former Soviet Union waged a ferocious campaign against it. The film makers of Hollywood are currently making strenuous efforts to discredit it … the list of intense opposition is long. And yet it remains the most widely read book in the world. It sells more copies than any other book, it is read in more languages than any other book. It has changed more lives and incited more testimonies of that change than any other book. More people have given their lives for it than for any other. Of the books of divine revelation the Bible is in a class of its own.

But the very idea of divine revelation is unacceptable to the secular humanist, and in fact to all atheists. There is no chance of consensus among the non-atheists either.

So concerning the question, "Do we know anything at all?" the conclusion that the only way that we can know anything is by faith is not a very satisfying answer for the philosopher, not a welcome answer for the scientist, not, in fact an answer very palatable to most people, but apparently the case nevertheless.

It would appear that the most important question is then:- Which faith is it wisest to put one's trust in?

Chapter 2

How Did It All Begin?

The question of origins and beginnings is of enormous importance. One's whole outlook on life depends on one's idea of how the universe and everything in it began. Among ancient cultures there were many stories of the beginning, almost all so incongruous and unsatisfying that they have long since been forgotten or are taken only as historical curiosities. But one ancient account still stands and still finds many adherents. One of the reasons for this is because it covers the whole subject in a consistent and credible manner. That account is the one found in the Bible. Until a century or so ago most of the educated people of the western world took this account as fact. The Biblical account says "In the beginning God created the heaven and the earth". It is clear from the genealogies of the Bible that this creation must have taken place just a few thousand years ago.

By the mid-nineteenth century James Hutton and Charles Lyell had popularised the idea of "Geological time", millions of years and purely natural processes replacing any idea of divine intervention. This changed the outlook of the civilised world on the whole question of origins. The philosophers and scientists began to seek an explanation in purely natural processes.

A point which must be realised is that such ideas are not really scientific. Science, as Mendeleev, Mach and Einstein pointed out, deals with what can be measured, everything else is speculation. Recorded human history goes back approximately five thousand years. No scientist can go back in time to take measurements of what happened before that, so when scientists make statements about anything that happened more than five thousand years ago they are dealing inevitably with speculation. The currently fashionable speculation on origins is known as the "Big Bang Theory".

In the beginning there was a "cosmic egg". Opinion differs among the Experts on just how big that egg was, some say smaller than the head of a pin, some say millions of kilometres in diameter, others make no statement of an actual size but just say that it was extremely dense. Many say it was a "quantum fluctuation", the size of which is so small as to be almost nonexistent! However, most seem to agree that about fifteen thousand million years ago it exploded and produced a gas called hydrogen. Some of the atoms of hydrogen collided and formed another gas, helium. The hydrogen and helium, together with little packets of energy called "photons", came shooting out of the explosion at great speed. As the ball of hot gas expanded it cooled. As it cooled it clumped together into clouds, which contracted, heated up and formed stars. Nuclear reactions in the stars produced "heavy" elements like oxygen, iron and carbon. Stars exploded manufacturing even heavier elements and scattering them all throughout the universe. Clouds of gas, enriched by these heavy elements contracted and formed, among other things, the sun, the planets and the earth.

Illustration 3
The currently popular idea of origins - an enourmous explosion.

The process continues with atoms, molecules and photons of energy combining by chance random processes to form plants, animals ... man.

Although this is known as the "Big Bang Theory", it does not actually merit the title "theory" on the scheme which science usually claims to follow. Rather, since there does not appear to be any way to test even one really significant point about this account by experiment, it ranks as a "hypothesis". This remarkable story seems to run counter to everyday experience. Experience tells us that any system left to itself runs down, becomes more random, less orderly, more chaotic. Yet here we see the order and complexity of the entire universe resulting from the total disorder of two gasses shooting out of an explosion. For science to have accepted an idea which runs completely counter to all experience we would presume that there is powerful evidence to support the idea, and a very good reason why it was put forward in the first place.

Scientists discovered that each element has a characteristic pattern of lines in its spectrum. Calcium, for example has three closely spaced red lines, one orange, one green and six blue lines in its visible spectrum. Astronomers examine the light coming from stars, and by finding the telltale patterns of lines, deduce what elements there may be in the outermost regions of stars. About a hundred years ago it was discovered that the patterns of lines were not always quite in the expected positions. The pattern was occasionally moved, or "shifted" slightly towards the blue part of the spectrum, or, more often, towards the red end of the spectrum. The only explanation that anyone seems to have been able to think of at that time was that a star with a blue shift must be moving towards the earth, one with a red shift must be moving away.

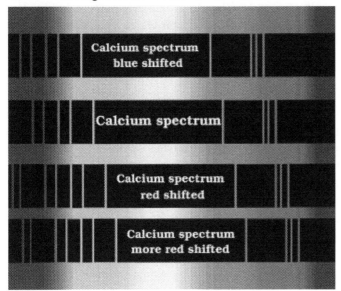

Calcium spectrum
blue shifted

Calcium spectrum

Calcium spectrum
red shifted

Calcium spectrum
more red shifted

Illustration 4

This pattern of
spectral lines
is the
"fingerprint" of
Calcium.

This is called the "Doppler Effect".

Besides stars, the astronomers discovered fuzzy patches of light which they deduced to be huge groups of stars. They were given the name "galaxies". Galaxies were usually found to have red shifts in their spectra. A puzzling relationship was noticed by an astronomer called Edwin Hubble. The fainter a galaxy (and therefore presumably the further away), the bigger the red shift in its spectrum (and therefore, presumably, the faster it must be moving away from the earth). An intriguing part about the observation was that it appeared to be so no matter where one looked. In every direction the distant galaxies seemed to be rushing away from the earth at great speed. The entire universe seemed to be expanding away from a centre, which to all appearances seemed to be the earth.

If the universe is expanding, then it must have been smaller in the past. If that is so, reasoned the scientists, then there must have been a time when all the material of the universe was at one point. The Big Bang was born.

This idea is, however, plagued with problems.

The cosmic egg is believed to have been denser than a "black hole", from which (those who believe in black holes tell us) nothing can escape, not even light. But everything in the universe escaped from this black hole.

Material shooting out of an explosion spreads out and disperses. The cloud of gas would simply get thinner and cooler. As Fred Hoyle pointed out, the Big Bang leads to "a dull-as-ditch-water expansion which degrades itself adiabatically until it is incapable of doing anything at all."[1] And yet the theory requires that this expanding gas clumps together into clouds, which contract to form galaxies, stars, planets and people. The originator of the theory, Lemaitre, speculated that the expansion must have stopped for long enough to allow the gas to clump together to form clouds. The clouds must have then started rushing on their way again. Most scientists have not been impressed with that idea. Where did the energy come from to stop the initial expansion? And where did the energy come from to set it all in motion again after the clumping together in clouds? So most accept no pause in the headlong rush from the explosion centre. How then did the material clump together instead of spreading out? Since no credible explanations have been put forward it has

---

1   Fred Hoyle, NEW SCIENTIST, Nov. 19, 1981 p. 523. ("adiabatically" = without addition of heat)

become necessary to believe that there were very special conditions in the explosion itself. Such theories give rise to the "anthropic principle", which states (in the version which makes any kind of sense at all), that the explosion must have been extremely carefully designed specifically to make the eventual existence of man possible. The other (more popular) version of the anthropic principle assumes that untold trillions of trillions of universes were formed, each with different properties, and ours just happened to have the right ones to allow the eventual appearance of man.

A cloud of gas at high temperature tends to fly apart. The theory requires that gravitational attraction between the molecules of gas pulls them together and makes the cloud contract. Calculations show that unless the temperature is less than five degrees absolute (minus two hundred and sixty-eight degrees Celsius) the thermal energy of the gas molecules tending to make the cloud disperse is greater than the gravitational energy tending to make it contract. So in order to start contracting, a cloud would have to be colder than five degrees absolute. Today there are clouds of gas in the universe from which astronomers say they believe stars are forming. The temperatures of these clouds have been measured. The temperatures are far too high, about a hundred degrees absolute, so they cannot be contracting (or forming stars) today. But the Big Bang tells us that in the past the temperature was higher. It would seem to have been even more impossible for them to have contracted in the past than today. To get over this impossibility "ad hocs" have to be brought in. A favourite is to assume that a star explodes near a cloud of gas and dust. Such an exploding star is called a "nova", or if bright enough, a "supernova". The explosion is supposed to make the cloud of gas and dust contract; but there seems to be no convincing reason why … such an explosion would logically make a nearby cloud disperse, not consolidate. There is a paradox in this theory. The star which exploded had to form long ago, when the expanding gas was hotter than today. It would therefore be even more difficult for the star which became the nova to form than for its explosion-generated successor.

The material shooting out of the Big Bang must have had enormous linear momentum, but the laws of mechanics show that it could not have had angular momentum, in other words this material must have been flying straight out of the explosion centre. Yet the astronomers are all agreed that the universe is full of bodies which are rotating and also moving around in circles (or rather ellipses). They have a great deal of angular momentum. Where did the angular momentum come from? This difficulty could be overcome by having several "Little Big Bangs" interacting with each other. Commenting on the possibility of little big bangs Hoyle noted:- "… the mathematics of little big bangs are more difficult to cope with than the mathematics of a single simple big bang".[2] He suggests that scientists would prefer to stick to theories whose mathematics they can handle, even if those theories are logically not very convincing.

The Big Bang is thought to have produced hydrogen and helium. The exact proportion can be juggled somewhat, a little under twenty percent helium is normally accepted. But once a figure has been chosen it must be taken as constant for the entire explosion. All the gas coming out of the Big Bang has the same proportion of helium. All the clouds have the same proportion, all the stars which form from those clouds have the same proportion. Now the theory goes on to say that nuclear reactions inside stars convert hydrogen into helium, so it would be quite possible to find stars with more helium than the assumed starting value, but there seems to be no way for the proportion to become less. Yet there is a class of "B-type" stars (bright, blue stars, which the astronomers believe to be "young") which have only about one percent of the required helium.[3] This would appear to be another contradiction to the theory.

Many problems have suggested that the Big Bang cannot be the correct explanation for the origin of the universe. Pondering the impossibilities, an American astronomer, Allan Guth, realised that he could get over some of them if the entire universe could have expanded vastly faster than the speed of light for part (but only part) of the early stages of the Big Bang. Practically all the scientists of the world accept that the speed of light is the limiting speed, they believe that nothing can exceed the speed of light. But Guth pointed out that having everything in the universe travelling many orders of magnitude faster than the speed of light for a short time could get the Big Bang out of the realm of indisputable impossibility. This idea is called "inflation". No phenomenon like it has ever been observed. No really plausible explanation has been put forward to explain how it could happen.

---

2 Fred Hoyle, THE INTELLIGENT UNIVERSE, Michael Joseph, London, 1983, p. 179.

3 D.W. Sciama, MODERN COSMOLOGY, pp. 150–153.

Inflation provides an insight into the way scientists sometimes overcome theoretical difficulties. Faced with evidence incompatible with a theory it is realised that if something else were true the theory would be able to survive. The "something else" is called an "ad hoc", it is brought in just to get over a particular difficulty for a theory. A scientist may then proceed to work out the consequences. Some ad hocs are soon seen to be useless, it becomes clear that they do not save the theory after all. But if the theory does seem to hang together, it becomes rather tempting to assume that the ad hoc might be true.

Almost all proponents of the Big Bang soon came to accept inflation (though recent difficulties have led many to abandon it again).

In the early stages of the Big Bang everything was supposed to be so hot that matter and energy could freely change places with each other. In astronomical jargon matter and energy were "coupled". But as the fireball expanded it must have got cooler very quickly and matter and energy would have "decoupled". The high energy radiation (photons) would then be free to hurtle off to infinity at the speed of light, never to be seen again by the matter left behind (inflation having come to an end). But this scenario is too dull to be of any value, so the theory keeps the energy within the universe by effectively having the universe contained in a perfectly reflecting balloon which expands as the light which tries to escape pushes it outwards. The theoreticians do not actually talk about a perfectly reflective coating to the universe, they actually talk about space itself expanding (an intriguing idea, which raises some awkward questions!). It is equivalent to a reflective elastic coating. Expansion leads to the temperature of the photons of energy falling. After sufficient time their temperature should have dropped until they are no longer visible, and they should have the frequency of microwaves. The Big Bang proponents calculated that this energy should have a range of energies (a "spectrum") of a certain kind, and an intensity, or strength, of a certain value.

In 1965 two scientists at the Bell Telephone Laboratories in America accidentally detected microwave radiation coming from all regions of the sky. They were almost instantly awarded a Nobel prize for providing the first and only "proof" of the Big Bang. The theory had predicted microwave radiation, but unfortunately the intensity of the radiation was about a hundred times less than predicted. It's temperature was also far lower than originally predicted (30 degrees Kelvin). The theorists brushed these problems aside in their desire to embrace the theory. There are several other explanations of the background radiation, but they are rarely mentioned. The first was put forward by Arthur Eddington in 1926 before the Big Bang had made any predictions at all. Eddington predicted that the temperature throughout space due to the radiation of starlight would be three degrees Kelvin. This is very close to the observed value.

There was a further problem with the "background" microwave radiation. It seemed to be absolutely uniform, "smooth" as the astronomers call it. Although it is difficult to see how stars, galaxies, etc. could actually form from an expanding cloud of gas, many had accepted that it could be possible if the initial distribution of mass in the explosion were not uniform but "lumpy". Observations suggest that the distribution of matter in the universe is very uneven, very lumpy. Such lumpiness should lead to unevenness in the background radiation, but it was smooth, far too smooth, apparently perfectly smooth. A satellite, the Cosmic Background Explorer Satellite (COBE for short), was built to examine this radiation in detail. COBE's readings also showed the background radiation to be perfectly smooth. An ingenious pattern of corrections and adjustments were later applied to COBE's readings. These produced tiny variations — a small fraction of a percent. The variations are smaller than the satellite's apparatus could have actually detected, and are therefore not very convincing. So little unevenness seems inadequate to explain the lumpiness of the universe. But some have resorted to artful speculation about the inflation period. Since the inflation period is outside the bounds of experimental testing, one is free to speculate unhindered by inconvenient facts or observations. With sufficient subtlety in devising ad hoc theories it seems that on the lumpiness issue the Big Bang is still credible for those who wish to believe it. There are other plausible explanations for a slight graininess of the background radiation, but they are rarely mentioned.[4]

Yet another difficulty for the theory comes from the red shifts which started the whole speculation. Problems with the Doppler shift interpretation arose as early as 1911 when it was found that the bright, blue "O" and "B" type stars in our region of the universe had much more red shift than they should have. Among these the very brightest and hottest, (the "O-type" stars") had twice the excess red shift of the "B" type stars. It is doubtful that anyone believed that the bright blues stars were racing away from the earth faster than the other stars, so it should have been admitted that the red shift must be caused by something other than the Doppler effect.. In stead it was given a name "the K effect", swept under the astronomical carpet and rarely men-

---

4 N.C. Wickramasinge, NATURE, Vol. 358, 13th August 1992, p. 547.

tioned again. More recently astronomers have uncovered a great deal of evidence that the red shifts are probably not due to motion. Chief among these scientists is the famous astronomer Halton Arp, who for a long time was a lone voice crying out against orthodoxy. He has been joined by other able scientists and his book, "Seeing Red" makes such a strong case that many more are likely to join him.[5] Even if the red shifts were due to motion it has been shown that such shifts could also occur from motions other than expansion. Another explanation, a fall in the speed of light, has much evidence to support it, but such an idea is very unpopular (it would upset many other cherished theories), and is usually ignored. A further problem comes from the most popular version of the Big Bang, which has space itself expanding between galaxies, rather than galaxies moving away from each other by flying through space. The problem is that such expansion should give a bigger red shift than actually observed, which leads to the conclusion that the universe is actually contracting, not expanding.

The truth appears to be that no one knows what causes the red shifts or whether the Universe is expanding, contracting, or maintaining the same size.

After surveying the scene, one is tempted to stand back and say "But why is the Big Bang hypothesis so widely accepted when there is so little evidence to support it and so much evidence against it." Even the scientists themselves seem to have known for a long time that it cannot be true. John Maddox, editor of the prestigious journal NATURE, in an article "Down With The Big Bang"[6] , said "In all respects save that of convenience, this view of the origin of the universe is thoroughly unsatisfactory". Leif Robinson, after pointing out three major problems said[7] :- "That trilogy was not designed to throw cold water on the state of astronomical knowledge. Rather, it attempts to focus on a problem — how to assimilate ever growing tidal waves of disparate information". His use of the term "disparate information" is a polite way of saying "evidence which disproves the popular theories of astronomy". And he acknowledged that there is not just a little evidence, but "ever growing tidal waves". Then why does the scientific establishment continue to propagate the Big Bang? There seems to be only one answer to that question. There

5 "Seeing Red" Halton Arp, Apeiron, Montreal, 1998

6 Maddox John, *Down With the Big Bang,* NATURE, Vol.340, 10th August, 1989.

7 Robinson L.J., *A Family Named Universe*, THE ASTRONOMY ENCYCLOPAE-DIA, Mitchel Beazley, 1987, p. 9

is no alternative which is philosophically acceptable to the scientists of the world. The philosophically acceptable alternatives which were proposed have been shown to be even worse from a scientific point of view than the Big Bang.

A few scientists are honest enough to change their ideas on what is philosophically acceptable. Fred Hoyle, for example, much against his inclination admitted "A component has evidently been missing from cosmological studies. The origin of the Universe, like the solution of the Rubik cube, requires an intelligence".[8]

Although he would hate to admit it, this great scientist — one of the few prepared to face the fact that he (and the other scientists) may have been wrong about fundamental issues — was lending support to the old paradigm of Creation. His conclusion fits in with the proposition that scientists used to believe before humanism took over, "In the beginning God created the Heaven and the Earth".

This simple statement, however, is not satisfying to those who have become accustomed to requiring a naturalistic explanation for everything. With science unable to send observers back in time to see what really did happen, the only possibility left for finding out about the origin of the universe would be to accept the authority of divine revelation — if it does indeed give any indication of how the universe was actually created. The scriptures are not very forthcoming, yet there does seem to be a clue on one aspect of the process that may have been used. In Isaiah 42 verse 5 it says that God "created the heavens and stretched them out". In Jeremiah 10 verse 12 it says he "stretched out the heavens by his discretion". This idea of "stretching out" is repeated in several other verses[9] so it is interesting to speculate on what the universe would look like if such a process had actually been used.

Many astronomical objects appear to be swirling round in the form of eddies. The Big Bang has no satisfactory explanation for the angular momentum revealed.

It is easy to see what happens in a "stretching out" process in any fluid — liquid or gas. One simply needs to fill a container with water, put one's hands together in the water, and stretch them out, or pull them apart. If there is a

---

8   Fred Hoyle, THE INTELLIGENT UNIVERSE, p. 189.

9   Isaiah 44 v.24; Zec.12 v. l; Psalm 104 v. 2; Isaiah 51 v.13; Jeremiah 51 v. 15 etc.

light above the water, then on the bottom one can see the shadows of eddies, little whirlpools, swirling round in the water. This is a characteristic feature of any stretching out process in fluids, it produces eddies. As we look out into the universe there appear to be many objects swirling around like eddies. There are millions of "spiral galaxies" which look exactly like the eddies produced in our little experiment with the bowl of water. One of them is even called the "Whirlpool Galaxy ".

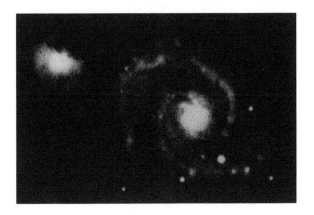

Illustration 5
The Whirlpool Galaxy
Many astronomical objects appear to be swirling round in the form of eddies.
The Big Bang has no satisfactory explanation for the angular momentum
revealed.

The angular momentum, the apparent tendency for everything to swirl around (which has no feasible explanation on the Big Bang theory), is a natural consequence of the process which the Bible suggests. It certainly appears more likely that a stretching out process rather than an explosion process was involved. But like all theories of origins it is not actually provable by science, all that science could do is to see if the predictions of such a process would fit the observed facts. But even if all the observations fit the idea we would still accept it or reject it on faith.

Any theory of origins can only be accepted by faith

Chapter 3

How Long Have We Been Here?

Estimates of the age of the earth, and the time that man has lived on it, have varied spectacularly over the last two hundred years. Throughout most of the first half of the 19th century geologists commonly believed the earth to be a few thousand years old. They believed that much of the sedimentary rock covering the earth's surface, layers of sediment clearly deposited in water, had been laid down very quickly in a major catastrophic flood. This interpretation is now known as "catastrophism". It was generally held that this event took place in the days of Noah.

James Hutton introduced the "Principle of Uniformitarianism" to geology with his catch phrase "The present is the key to the past" in about 1785. Little attention was paid to his idea at the time, but following in his footsteps Charles Lyell, the "father of modern geology" (who was born on the day Hutton died), popularised the idea to the extent that it became the foundational idea of geology. He expressed it formally in his textbook "Principles of Geology" like this:-

"No causes have, from the earliest time to which we can look back to the present, ever acted but those now acting, and they have never acted with degrees of energy different to which they now exert".

Although called a "principle", it is actually speculation — it claims to look back to a time before the earliest available written records. Although unverified it rapidly gained acceptance and became generally considered a self evident truth on which the whole of historical geology has been built. Geologists have now been forced to recognise that the uniformity principle is not true. They have discreetly replaced Lyell's .principle by a statement that the laws of nature have remained constant over time. This does not allow any estimation of ages. Those based on Lyell's principle are however maintained as sacrosanct even though now they are without any justification. The most important consequence of Lyell's principle was that vast ages of time would have been required to build up deposits of sedimentary rock. Observations today show that silt is being laid down on the deep ocean floors at a very slow rate, such a slow rate that it would take millions of years to build up the sediment now covering the earth.

Within a few years geologists had raised their estimates of the age of the earth and the time that man has been on it drastically. We might well ask, is it actually important to know the true age? A geologist may hold a piece of rock in his hand and pronounce it to be a hundred million years old. A pre-Lyellian geologist might have pronounced the same rock to have been, say, five thousand years old. Who is to say which is right, or indeed if either guess is anywhere near the truth? And does it really matter anyway? Probably for most purposes not very much. But there are some situations where it is not just a question which can be left to personal preference. There are actually pressing reasons why we should be confident of the real time scale. The problem of safe storage of nuclear wastes (which are extremely dangerous for hundreds of thousands of years) is one which is so serious that a rock-solid foundation is required for design. This was brought home forcefully by the Chernobyl disaster; the consequences of leakage of nuclear material in that case were drastic. As a civil engineer this is a matter of professional importance to me personally, but it is not only important to engineers, or to the scientists and politicians who make the decisions on such matters. I have spent time in the area affected by the Chernobyl disaster. Most of the people I came across who were affected by that disaster were not engineers — or scientists — or politicians, but ordinary people. Most of the seriously affected were children. The most seriously affected were babies.

Structural Engineering design involves estimates of safety. A factor of safety is accepted such that there is perhaps one chance in a million that failure will occur in the life of the structure. To establish the safety factor for the structure it is necessary to estimate the worst conditions likely to be encountered in its working life — the worst floods, the strongest winds, the most severe earthquakes and so on. The only way of making such estimates is to look back into the past (preferably much further back than one working lifetime) and see what floods, winds, earthquakes, etc. have happened previously. Most engineering structures have a design life of less than a hundred years. Looking back a few hundred years normally presents little problem. But for a structure which must remain safe for hundreds of thousands of years we need to look back well beyond the five thousand years of recorded history and into the time of uniformitarian speculation.

When this problem of the design of nuclear waste storage structures arose in America a number of years ago a conference was called at the Civil Engineering Department of Louisiana State University. The aim of the conference was to examine the evidence for the generally accepted history of the earth and see whether it was reliable enough to take as a basis for design. The results of the symposium were written up in the well-known journal "Geotimes" in an article "It's About Time"[1] . Before looking at that report, we should note firstly that it is practically unheard of for "respectable" journals of science to allow suspicions of the time scale to be mentioned (such a paper is a "once in a lifetime" event), and secondly that many pieces of evidence had indeed been discovered which threw doubt on the reliability of the accepted geological time scale.

For example there is the problem of the helium in the earth's atmosphere. Helium is being produced by nuclear decay in the rocks of the earth, it is also being produced in the atmosphere itself. Thousands of tons are being added every year to the atmosphere. If the earth really were very old there ought to be a great deal of helium in the atmosphere, but there is not; there is only enough helium to account for a very much younger age.[2] Attempts to explain this away by assuming that helium could escape into space backfired, because there are two kinds or "isotopes" of helium, the normal Helium-4 and a lighter kind, Helium-3. Any escape mechanism would allow Helium-3 to escape more easily than Helium-4. The observed proportion of Helium-3 is so large that the estimate of age has had to be reduced, not increased. Any escape mechanism would mean that the atmosphere would be even younger.

In the atmosphere there is also Carbon-14, which is being produced by cosmic radiation from nitrogen. The rate at which this process is going on has been measured. The amount in the atmosphere has also been measured, and it appears that there is enough to account for this process going on for only a few thousand years.

---

1 Kasman R., GEOTIMES, Sept. 1978, pp. 18–20.

2 Cook M., *Where is the Earth's Radiogenic Helium?*, NATURE, Jan.26, 1957, p. 213.

There is also the problem of the earth's magnetic field. It is generally agreed that the main component, the symmetric dipole component (the component that makes a compass needle point to the North) is produced by electric currents circulating in the earth's iron core. Any such current would require a power source to keep it running. It needs some kind of a dynamo mechanism. The only power source that has ever been found for any such dynamo is the collapsing flux of the magnetic field itself. Analysis of the observed flux shows that it cannot have provided power for more than a few thousand years. There have been proposals that there may be some other power source, but since no one has found a feasible one yet, it remains unverified speculation. Analysis of the situation actually known to exist suggests that the earth cannot have had a magnetic field for more than just a few thousand years.[3]

Illustration 6

The main component of the earth's magnetic field causes a compass needle to point to the North. The field is dying away so quickly that in less than 2 000 years it will be too weak to do so anymore, and a compass needle will point in the direction of local magnetic "noise".

Then there is the problem of meteoric dust. When fairly large pieces of material from space tear into the atmosphere they heat up because of friction and

3   Barnes T., THE ORIGIN AND DESTINY OF THE EARTH'S MAGNETIC FIELD, ICR Technical monograph No 4.

Note that "field reversals" are no refutation. As Humphreys has shown, the only feasible mechanism dissipates energy rapidly. His mechanism calls for reversals to take pace very quickly, a prediction borne out by the work of Coe and Prevot, see Earth and Planetary Sciences Letters, 92(1989)292-298.

become visible as meteors or "shooting stars". Fine dust however, is slowed down so quickly that it does not get burned up, it drifts slowly down onto the earth. That which falls on the land surface gets washed into the rivers, the rivers flow into the oceans. Meteoric dust is rich in nickel, whereas the rocks of the Earth are very poor in this metal. An assessment has been done of how much nickel is being carried in solution by rivers, and how much is in solution in the oceans; the amounts measured suggest that the process has been going on for only a few thousand years.

There are many other indications that the earth is very young, for example the pressure observed in many oil wells is such that if the oil fields were millions of years old then the oil should have dissipated through the pores and cracks in the rock. To be still in existence, oil fields cannot be very old. The concentrations of many of the dissolved minerals in the oceans, when compared to the observed rate of addition by rivers suggest a very young age. Population dynamics suggest a very short duration for man's existence on earth.

With much evidence against the idea of a great age for the earth, where does the confidence expressed by conventional geology spring from?

Widespread confidence in the great ages seems to depend very largely on radiometric dating. The fundamental idea in radiometric dating is that certain atomic nuclei are unstable, a nucleus occasionally splits to become the nucleus of a different kind of element. Although it cannot be predicted when any particular atom will disintegrate, on average it seems to occur at a set rate. That rate can be expressed as a "half life", which is the time it takes for half of the atoms present to undergo decay. The fundamental radiometric dating method in geology is Uranium/Lead. Uranium decays by a complicated series of steps to become a stable kind of lead. It is assumed that if that kind of lead is found with uranium in a rock, the lead came from uranium originally. The time needed to produce the observed proportions can be calculated. It has to be assumed that the processes occurring in rock over an unknown (but long) period are the same as those occurring in strictly controlled conditions in a laboratory for a short time. It has to be assumed that it is valid to extrapolate back millions of years from laboratory tests lasting a few months.

For some time Uranium/Lead was considered a reliable dating method. But it soon became clear that there are problems with it. For a start there are many assumptions which may not be at all reasonable.

The first assumption is that when the material is thrown out in a volcanic eruption, any lead produced by previous decay when the lava was still inside the earth is separated from the uranium by movement of the fluid lava. The atomic clock is thus "reset" to zero. One must also assume that after the lava solidifies to form rock there is no movement of material in or out. There are many other assumptions, but just this one, that nothing moves in or out, was addressed by Henry Faul, who said:- "Uranium and Lead both migrate in geologic time, and detailed analyses have shown that useful ages cannot be obtained with them. ... widely divergent ages can be measured on samples from the same spot."[4] That throws serious doubt on how much reliance we can place on Uranium/Lead ages.

Melvin Cook analysed some of the most important Uranium deposits in the world, in Katanga and in Alaska and his findings also throw doubt on the method. He pointed out that the observed ratios of isotopes do not agree with theoretical predictions, and suggested that a neutron capture mechanism could explain the discrepancy. Such a mechanism would invalidate all Uranium-Thorium dates.[5]

Whether he is right or not in saying that the problem is due to neutron capture is a question which could only be settled by detailed long-term research, but what is clear is that the whole question of exactly what has happened in radioactive decay processes in rocks in the field is far from certain.

For a time the Potassium Argon method was considered reliable, but then it was discovered that huge discrepancies occur. Often dates are vastly younger or older than expected. This is not surprising since argon is a gas which is abundant in the air and the rocks. It is mobile, and can move quite easily through rock. It is by no means certain that the argon that one finds in association with potassium came from decay of that potassium. It is not uncommon to find a thousand times more (or less) argon than there should be. Results are accepted or rejected purely on whether they fit the age that was expected before the test was performed.[6]

The Rubidium Strontium method was for quite a long time considered reli-

4 Faul H., AGES OF ROCKS PLANETS AND STARS, McGraw Hill, 1966.

5 Cook M., PREHISTORY AND EARTH MODELS, Max Parish, 1960.

6 Hyatsu A., CANADIAN JOURNAL OF EARTH SCIENCES, vol 193, 17 Sept.1976,p.1093

able. It seems to give more consistent ages for a particular sample than the other methods. But ages are not necessarily reliable just because they are reasonably consistent. In fact there are a number of problems. For example Strontium-87, on which the method depends, can be produced from Rubidium-87 by the emission of an electron, but it can also be produced from Strontium-86 by neutron capture. Strontium-87 is mobile, it is not possible to tell whether the Strontium-87 in a sample came from Rubidium-87 or from Strontium-86 (or, indeed, from some other source). Experts admit that the method is unreliable, as Brooks, James and Hart pointed out[7], "... crystallization ages determined on basic igneous rocks by the Rb-Sr whole-rock technique can be greater than the true age by many hundreds of millions of years. This problem of inherited age is more serious for younger rocks, and there are well-documented instances of conflicts between stratigraphic age and Rb-Sr age in the literature."

There is one radiometric dating method which is not dependent on quite so many tentative assumptions. That is the Radio-Halo method. In this method a small group of radioactive atoms is examined in conjunction with the pattern formed in the surrounding rock by the helium nuclei (usually called alpha particles) ejected during the decay processes. A cross-section through a radioactive centre in rock reveals circles around the nucleus. These are called "radio-haloes"; they actually represent cross sections through spheres, at the centre of which is the group of radioactive atoms. At each stage in the decay process the alpha particles are thrown out with a very specific energy, so they reach specific distances as they shoot into the surrounding rock. Since every stage has its own energy, each stage forms a sphere of a specific radius. It is possible to identify which "halo" was produced by the decay of Uranium-238, which was from Radium-226, which was from Polonium-218, and so on. The various kinds of atoms remaining at the centre can be identified and counted.

The world's leading expert on radio-haloes, Robert V Gentry, was invited to address the symposium at Louisiana State University. He pointed out that ages indicated by radio-halo analysis can be far less than those generally accepted. The report on his presentation said:- "If isotope ratios are to be used as a basis for geologic dating then presently accepted ages may be too

---

7 C.Brooks, D.E.James, S.R.Hart, SCIENCE, vol 193, 17 Sept. 1976,p.1093

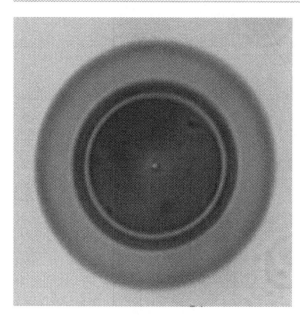

Illustration 7

Radio halo analysis probably gives more insight than other radiometric dating methods. Each circle corresponds to the decay of one particular radioactive stage in the decomposition. The method suggests far younger ages than popularly believed.

Photo R.V.Gentry

high by a factor of 10 000 … Thus ages of the entire stratigraphic column may contain epochs less than 0.01% the duration of those now accepted and found in the literature."[8] That could have great significance for the factor of safety in the design of nuclear waste storage plants.

Geologists often admit that there are many uncertainties in geologic dating, and many indications of a young age; but they point out that astronomers assure us that the earth must be thousands of millions of years old, so the evidence for a far younger age can be ignored.

Astronomers were also invited to speak at the symposium at L.S.U. Some of their contributions are touched upon in Chapter 5. The message from them was that there are indeed theories in astronomy which present great ages, but observational support is conspicuous by its absence. Dr. John Eddy, one of the world's leading experts on the sun, said at that symposium:- "I suspect … that the sun is 4.5 billion years old. However, given some new and unexpected results to the contrary, and some time for frantic readjustment, I sus-

---

8 GEOTIMES, Sept. 1977, p.19.

For a full discussion of Radiohaloes and their indication of a very short timescale see Robert V. Gentry's CREATIONS'S TINY MYSTERY, Earth Science Associates, Knoxville, Tennessee

pect that we could live with Bishop Ussher's value for the age of the Earth and Sun. I don't think we have much in the way of observational evidence in astronomy to conflict with that."

Bishop Ussher's estimate for the age of the earth was about six thousand years. According to one of the world's leading experts, astronomers do not have real observational evidence that the earth is actually any older than that. The implications for the safety of a long term structure like a nuclear waste storage plant are radical. An engineer making a design on which the lives of thousands (perhaps millions) of people depend ought to ask for more than just the suspicions of astronomical theorists.

Since the popularly accepted geological ages cannot be reliably supported by radiometric dating or astronomical observation we ought to ask what evidence does actually support them? Where does the geological time scale come from?

The part of the column in which no fossils of complex creatures have been found (the Precambrian) is indeed dated by radiometric dating. Its dates are therefore totally speculative and unreliable. That the scientists themselves recognise this unreliability can be seen from the statement by William Stansfield[9] :- "It is obvious that radiometric techniques may not be the absolute dating methods that they are claimed to be. Age estimates on a given geological stratum by different radiometric methods are often quite different (sometimes by hundreds of millions of years)." and also from that by Frederic Jeuneman[10] :- "There has been in recent years the horrible realisation that radio decay rates are not as constant as previously thought, nor are they immune to environmental influences. And this could mean that the atomic clocks are reset during some global disaster, and events which brought the Mesozoic to a close may not be 65 million years ago but, rather, within the age and memory of man."

The events which brought the Mesozoic to a close are supposed to have brought the extinction of the dinosaurs. Jeuneman is here suggesting that they are

---

9 Stansfield W.D., THE SCIENCE OF EVOLUTION, Macmillan, New York, 1977, p.84.

10 Jeuneman F.B., FAIC, *Secular catastrophism*, INDUSTRIAL RESEARCH AND DEVELOPMENT, June 1982, p.21.

within the memory of man, in other words, man and dinosaurs lived at the same time. There seems to be a good deal of evidence to support this possibility, there is even evidence that they may have been exterminated by man because they were dangerous and a nuisance. But be that as it may, he is giving clear recognition of the fact that radiometric dating methods are invalid. It seems inconsistent, to say the least, to accept radiometric ages for the Pre-Cambrian part of the geological column when they are known to be valueless for the more recent section.

The part of the column containing readily recognisable fossils, the Cambrian and later, is not dated by radiometric methods, it is dated by the fossils. Geologists and palaeontologists often have radiometric dates taken, but if they do not agree with the stratigraphic age they are discarded. If they do agree they are accepted as confirming the age that had already been decided upon. The basis for the stratigraphic dating method was pointed out by O.H. Schindewolf when he said[11] "The only chronometric scale applicable in geological history for the stratigraphic classification of rocks and for dating geological events exactly is furnished by the fossils. Owing to the irreversibility of evolution, they offer an unambiguous time scale for relative age determinations and for world-wide correlation of rocks."

It is the interpretation of the fossil record in terms of Lyell's uniformity principle and the theory of evolution which gives the time scale.

But the theory of evolution relies on this very interpretation in the first place! This can be seen in the admission by Carl Dunbar[12] :- "fossils provide the only historical documentary evidence that life has evolved from simpler to more and more complex forms."

There are strong grounds for suspecting that this evidence is highly dubious. The theory of evolution is on very shaky ground from many points of view.

Charles Darwin said of the fossil record[13] that it was "... the most obvious

---

11 Schindewolf O.H., AMERICAN JOURNAL OF SCIENCE, vol. 255, June 1957, p.395.

12 Dunbar C.O. HISTORICAL GEOLOGY, John Wiley & Sons, Inc., New York, 1960, p.47.

13 Darwin C., *On the Imperfections of the Geological Record,* THE ORIGIN OF SPECIES, J.M Dent & Sons, London, 1971, p.293.

and serious objection which can be urged against the theory". Mark Ridley of Oxford University said of it[14] "... the false idea that the fossil record provides an important part of the evidence that evolution took place. In fact, evolution is proven by a totally separate set of arguments". It should be noted that this expert says "arguments" establish the theory of evolution, not the fossil record. It is only when the geological record has been interpreted in terms of the theory of evolution in the first place that it then supports evolution. As pointed out by Ronald West of Kansas State University[15] "Contrary to what most scientists write, the fossil record does not support the Darwinian theory of evolution because it is this theory (there are several) which we use to interpret the fossil record. By doing so we are guilty of circular reasoning if we then say the fossil record supports the theory". Just how circular we can see in the admission by J.E. O'Rourke[16] "The procession of life was never witnessed, it is inferred. The vertical sequence of fossils is thought to represent a process because the enclosing rocks are interpreted as a process. The rocks do date the fossils, but the fossils date the rocks more accurately. Stratigraphy cannot avoid this kind of reasoning, if it insists on using only temporal concepts, because circularity is inherent in the derivation of time scales."

In order to get away from the circular (and therefore invalid) interpretations which have dominated geological thinking for many years it is necessary to examine not only the fossils but also the popular preconceptions associated with them.

Fossils are the preserved remains of plants and animals which have turned into rock by the replacement of tissue with minerals. Several other phenomena are also called fossils. For example a preserved imprint (such as a footprint) may be called a fossil, a creature (usually an insect) preserved in the resin which seeps out of a tree like a pine is called a fossil, an organism preserved in ice can also be called a fossil. But the petrified remains of organisms themselves are the most intriguing, and perhaps the most important. Contrary to popular misconception, no one knows how they formed. According to the commonly accepted scheme of the geological time scale, fossils of

---

14 Mark Ridley, *Who doubts Evolution*, NEW SCIENTIST,June 1981, p.830.

15 West, R. *Paleoecology and Uniformitarianism*, COMPAS, May 1968, p.216.

16 J.E.O'Rourke, AMERICAN JOURNAL OF SCIENCE, vol. 276, Jan 1976, p.47 & p.53.

clearly recognisable creatures appear for the first time in a period called the Cambrian. Prior to this there are usually no fossils, except for possibly bacteria, and perhaps even spores.

It is usually stated that fossils form when a creature dies, falls to the ground (or sinks to the bottom of the sea), and becomes covered with sediments, sand, silt, etc. which gradually build up to a great depth. Minerals in the water of the soft sediments percolate into the dead creature and replace the tissue. After very many years the sediments have built up to such a thickness that the

Illustration 8
The Coelacanth, extinct for more than 60 million years according to the
uniformitarian interpretation of the fossil record, is still alive and well.

pressure is great enough to turn the mineralised creature and the sediment around it to stone. It is believed that this is a purely random process, and although only a small proportion (the usual estimate, or rather, guess, is one in a million) of the population actually becomes fossilised, with enough time some members of any population are almost certain to be preserved like this. Thus if a population existed during a particular period, some of its members would almost certainly be preserved in the record. One can tell what creatures were alive during any period by the presence of their fossils.

That foundational assumption received a severe blow in 1938 when a coelacanth was landed at East London, on the East Coast of South Africa. The coelacanth disappeared from the geological column at the end of the

Mesozoic era. It became extinct, according to the accepted interpretation of the fossil record, sixty-five million years ago after it evolved into an amphibian. And yet it is still alive, having existed through the entire Cainozoic era without leaving any trace in the fossil record.

Many other "extinct" creatures have been found. Solendon, a little shrew-like mammal, for example, disappeared from the fossil record thirty-five million geological years ago. It is still in existence.

The same is true for the tuatara, which looks like a lizard with a beak-shaped head. There is no trace in the fossil record since the middle of the Mesozoic. It supposedly became extinct a hundred and thirty million years ago, yet it clearly did not, it has been alive and well throughout the whole period it was missing from the record.

Lingula, a small marine creature, was supposed to have become extinct five hundred million years ago, since it disappeared from the fossil record just after the Cambrian period. It is still alive today, having existed throughout practically the whole of the Palaeozoic, the whole of the Mesozoic, and the whole of the Cainozoic eras without leaving a trace in the fossil record. Like all the other "living fossils", it does not show any trace of having evolved at all in that supposed vast length of time. Lingula testifies strongly to the fact that the uniformitarian interpretation of the fossil record is unacceptable.

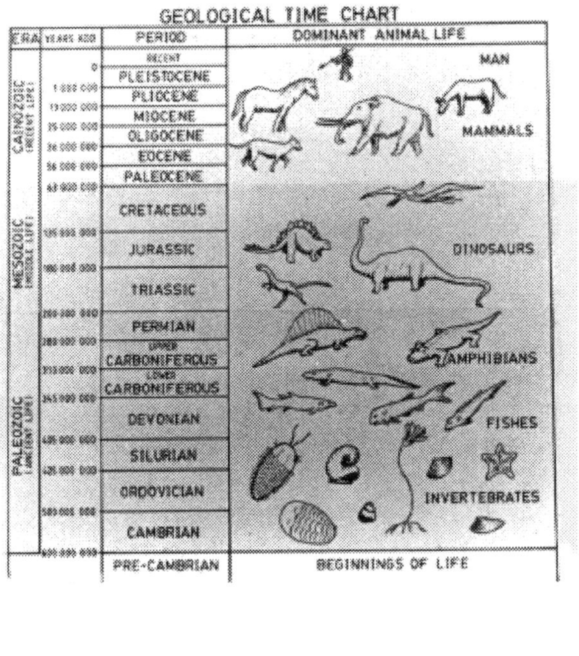

Illustration 9
The interpretation of the fossil record in terms of uniformity and evolution led to the Geological Column, with its ages and eras of millions of years. The Pre-Cambrian, which is supposed to have lasted thousands of millions of years, has few, if any fossils.

There are serious problems with the fossil record of plants also. The angiosperms (flowering plants) are widely stated to have evolved just before the time of the dinosaurs. However angiosperm remains have been found in Carboniferous rock which is supposed to be very much older, and some even admit fossilised flowering plants in the Cambrian period. Even more intriguing, pollen has apparently been found in the Hakatai Shale beds of the Grand Canyon.[17]

This rock is Pre-Cambrian, no "advanced" plants or animals should have been in existence in that period. The pollen comes from trees like maple and oak. Fossils of such trees are found only in much later periods — hundreds of millions of years later according to the geological time scale. Since oak and maple pollen is produced only by oak and maple trees, it looks as if such trees were in existence for a large part of geological history without leaving one fossilised specimen. The uniformitarian interpretation again appears more like speculation than history.

Illustration 10 : Foraminifera
These tiny single-called creatures with shells are often used as "Index fossils"
to identify a particular age of rock, but they are sometimes found in rocks of the
"wrong" age!

---

17 Howe G.F., Williams G.T., Lammerts W.E., CRSQ Vol 24, March 1988, pp.173-182.

There are other problems with the usual interpretation. Certain fossils are used to specifically indicate particular periods. One of the most important types of index fossil is a group called "foraminifera" — single celled creatures with shells. Particular kinds of foraminifera are associated with particular geological periods. But it happens that foraminifera are found in the wrong layers, they are sometimes found in layers which are assigned ages different to those for which they are supposed to be indicators. When this happens a geologist will usually say it is an example of "displacement" (a fossil in the wrong place).[18]

The use of a technical term then seems to obscure the fact that such an occurrence undermines the validity of the whole interpretation. In the case of foraminifera, kinds said to be specific to one time period being found in rocks assigned to another period may not seem very glamorous, but there are other anomalies which are considerably more dramatic, and more obviously raise great problems for the uniformitarian interpretation.

A good example is a piece of sandstone taken out of a quarry near the town of London in Texas. The quarry material used to be classified as Ordovician

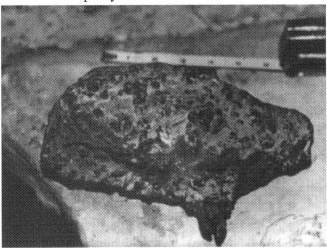

Illustration 11
Triassic (formerly Ordovician !) sandstone with a piece of partially coalified spruce embedded.

---

18   Foraminifera have been found in the wrong place in embarrassing circumstances so often, that some have now changed their mind about the irreversibility of evolution and say that foraminifera must have evolved back and forth between the various kinds repeatedly.

sandstone, with an assumed age of about four to five hundred million years. It was later re-classified as Triassic with a much younger age. The sandstone had been dated by pelecipod fossils characteristic for the Ordovician period. But sticking out of the sandstone is a piece of fossilised (partially coalified) wood.

Examination has shown that it is actually spruce. But spruce is not supposed to have evolved until millions of years after the Ordovician period. This piece of rock contains an even more severe anomaly — the coalified spruce can be seen to be the remains of the handle of an iron hammer. The only creature known to have ever made iron hammers with spruce handles is man, and according to the standard interpretation he is not supposed to have arrived on the scene till millions of years after spruce trees ... and vastly later than the shellfish of the Ordovician period - or the dinosaurs of the Triassic. Surprisingly, many scientists are prepared to dismiss all such evidence as "artifact" without even considering their detailed chemical and physical analyses. This is even more surprising in view of the general unwillingness to accept that archaeopteryx could be an artifact, despite a serious challenge by well-known scientists and the refusal of museum authorities to allow any chemical tests at all.[19]

The story of the fossils is in severe doubt. This is hardly surprising since no one actually knows how fossils form. The commonly repeated hypothesis which was mentioned earlier is simply conjecture. No one has ever been able to observe fossilisation happening in this way anywhere in the world. Scientists have examined sites where they think fossils ought to be forming, and they have tried to produce fossils in this way in the laboratory, but they have never succeeded (though petrification has been observed to happen in a matter of days by bacterial action.). They have succeeded in producing examples of the other phenomena which are also called fossils, such as preserved impressions. The problem is that when a creature dies it is always either eaten by scavengers or destroyed by agents of putrefaction. Even in cases of preservation in hot volcanic ash, water subsequently seeping through has brought bacteria, fungi, and other agents of decay which have destroyed the original organism, so that only a hollow "cast" is left where the organism used to be.

19 R.S.Watkins, F.Hoyle, N.C.Wickramasinghe, J.Watkins, R.Rabilizirov and L.M.Spetner, *Archaeopteryx - A Photographic Study*, BRITISH JOURNAL OF PHOTOGRAPHY, March 8th 1985 and two subsequent issues.

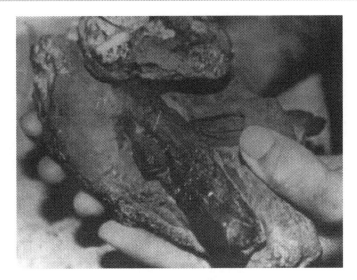

Illustration 12
The partially coalified spruce is the handle of an iron hammer.

Since a "real" fossil has never been observed to form in the way the geological story requires, it is obvious that we cannot be at all certain that fossils actually did form that way. In which case it is not at all certain that fossils do tell us what we have always assumed that they tell us.

There are many cases of fossilised tree trunks standing vertically in horizontally bedded sediments which have apparently been laid down on top of each other in water. It is not uncommon to find tree trunks ten metres long preserved in this way. Historical geology requires many thousands of years for ten metres of sediment to be deposited. It is a fact of experience that a tree trunk standing in sediment rots quickly, yet such trees show no sign of decay anywhere along their length. This fact is sometimes explained by assuming that the tree trunks must have fossilised somewhere else, perhaps in a horizontal position, and later been transported to the present site. But even if it were possible for a tree to fossilise in a horizontal position without any decay, a ten metre long fossilised tree trunk could hardly stand upright for thousands of years while sediment gradually built up to cover it, it would have fallen over. Such fossils suggest that the deposits must have built up vastly quicker than the popular theories of geology assume.

Many other kinds of fossils suggest not only very rapid burial, but also rapid fossilisation. There are for example, well-known fossils of large fish in the

Illustration 13
Tree trunks standing vertically in horizontally bedded strata suggest very rapid
burial.

process of swallowing small fish, the shape of the body in some cases showing quite clearly that muscular activity was going on as the predator thrust
itself forward to swallow its prey. They appear to have been engulfed very
quickly in so much sediment that further movement became immediately
impossible. Fish protein is particularly prone to rapid putrefaction, and yet
both diner and dinner are perfectly preserved, each scale and fin in place.
Even if the fish had been rapidly buried by, for example, a mud slide, agents
of decay, which seem to live everywhere, even in the mud at the bottom of the
ocean, would soon have caused decomposition. Since the agents of decay
had no time to destroy the fish it looks as if not only burial but also fossilisation must have been very rapid.

Dinosaurs also testify to extremely rapid burial. Many dinosaur fossils have
been found with the huge creatures in upright positions, some in such an
attitude that they appear to have been swimming when they were suddenly
engulfed by vast quantities of sediment. If sediments were actually laid down
at the rate usually assumed, a dead dinosaur would have had to remain on its
feet, with its head high, immune to the attention of scavengers and bacteria,
for very many years while it was gradually covered by sediment. Another
fact about dinosaur remains belies the millions of years ago story. Unfossilised
bones have been found containing blood and DNA. DNA decomposes very

quickly after death -this is a major problem for genetic engineering and many of the patents that genetic engineering firms squabble about concern this very problem. The rate at which DNA breaks down has been measured, the DNA in dinosaur bones has been analysed. It is possible to estimate haw long it took for the observed degeneration of dino-DNA to have occurred. The bones can not be more than a few thousand years old even stretching things to the limits of feasibility. Blood cells can also not survive for vast ages without decomposition. They also testify that the bones are not millions of years old.

Fossil graveyards occur at various places in the world. Here millions of creatures have been swept together and fossilised *en masse*. The existence of thousands of millions of fossils which clearly all formed at the same time is quite astounding when one considers that no such fossils have ever been observed to form in our own time. It would appear that some very special conditions were needed for fossilisation, conditions which do not occur today. Without understanding those special conditions it is hard to see how much confidence can be placed in any interpretation of the fossil record.

It is usually assumed that if two fossilised creatures are found close together, then the creatures must have lived close to each other. And if one is found above another it must have lived later. But often fossils show creatures dismembered, the skull torn from the body, even the strong rigid skull distorted. Such appearance is consistent with the creatures having been carried by extremely violent currents of water, in which case the fact that they were deposited together would not necessarily mean that they lived together. And since deposition in turbulent water tends to follow the pattern of first small regular bodies, then large regular bodies, then small irregular bodies and finally large irregular bodies, then the order in which fossils are found might have more to do with hydrodynamic sorting than chronology.

The geological record contains other things besides fossils, a very interesting item being meteorites. Meteorites are chunks of material which were formerly hurtling through space, but whose path happened to bring them in contact with the Earth. Unlike the smaller, more common such pieces — meteors (which burn up completely as they race through the atmosphere), meteorites are large enough to reach the surface of the earth without being completely burned up. Today about six hundred meteorites strike the earth every year, many of them fall into the sea, but about one hundred and fifty strike the land surface. Practically all astronomers believe there were more meteorites in the past than there are today, many have already been "swept up", not only by the earth and the planets, but also by the sun, so the meteorite population of the solar system is dwindling. Many of them are made of stainless steel — they are called "nickel-iron" meteorites; others are made of rocky material. The section of the geological record which contains fossils of clearly recognisable creatures begins with the period called the Cambrian. But throughout the whole record from the Cambrian to the Recent not one meteorite has ever been found. This period is commonly believed to have lasted for six hundred million years, so at least three hundred and sixty thousand-million meteorites should be expected to be found in this section of the record — they should be very common. And yet not a single meteorite has ever been found from the Cambrian to the mid Quaternary (which is right at the top of the column). If the geological time scale were correct at least a hundred should have been found in the coal mined in the last century alone. None have been found. A few meteorites have been found at the boundary of the Cambrian and the Pre-Cambrian. In addition, this boundary looks like a recognisable old land surface with similar features to those known today on the land surface — a very rare occurrence in the geological record. On the whole the meteorites do not seem to fit in well with the story usually told. They suggest that the period from the Cambrian to the Recent was of short duration.

Illustration 14
The Hobba meteorite is the largest in the world. In the foreground can be seen two places where souvenir hunters have tried to chip pieces off. They are bright and shiny, showing no trace of rust. The meteorite is of stainless steel.

Yet another feature of the record is preserved impressions, for example footprints. Experimentally it seems that the only way to preserve footprints as found in the fossil record is to make impressions (preferably under water) and cover them immediately with sediment. Otherwise the imprints disappear very quickly. There are famous footprints, apparently of men and dinosaurs, at several places in the world. The best known are at the Paluxy River in Texas. When they were first exposed and very clear they were ignored by evolutionists. Secular humanist scientists only began to pay them attention after considerable erosion, by which time they had become rather indistinct. Since then a controversy has raged over their genuineness. Russian scientists have found tracks of men and dinosaurs together in Siberia. Even "older", geologically, are large numbers of human footprints found in Carboniferous rock in many places in America. The age of the rock is supposed to be about two hundred and fifty million years. Commenting on these footprints[20] Albert Ingalls refused to accept the possibility of their having been made by the feet of men, because otherwise "the whole science of geology is so completely wrong that all the geologists will resign their jobs and take up truck driving". Ingalls, however seems to have missed the fact that the science of geology — that which is based on measurement and observation, and which makes geology economically valuable — is on a sound footing, it is only the speculations of Historical Geology which are in serious doubt.

There are, then, good reasons to believe that the interpretation of the geological record in terms of Lyell's uniformity principle has major flaws. This is not surprising since most of the scientific community is now confident that the earth has been struck by at least one major meteorite of at least ten kilometres in diameter. Analysing such an impact O'Keefe and Ahrens of the California Institute of Technology pointed out[21], that such an impact would have had the power of a thousand-million-megaton bomb, and if it landed in the ocean it would vaporise about ten million-million tons of water, which would soon condense and fall as rain. It would also have thrown up a similar quantity of water as liquid, some of it with sufficient velocity to go into orbit around the earth. They calculated that whether the meteorite fell in the ocean or on land it would have produced an earthquake a million times more powerful than

---

20 Ingalls Albert G., *The Carboniferous Mystery*, SCIENTIFIC AMERICAN, Vol. 162, Jan 1940 p.14.

21 O'Keefe John D. and Ahrens Thomas J., *Impact mechanics of the Cretaceous-Tertiary extinction bolide*, NATURE, Vol. 298, 8 July, 1982, pp.123-127. Also *Did Tidal Wave Kill Dinosaurs*, Report on Ahrens T.J. and O'Keefe J.D., 13th. Lunar and Planetary Sciences Conference, AstroNews, ASTRONOMY, June 1982, pp.62-64

severe earthquakes experienced today, and that this earthquake would have raised tidal waves five kilometres high which would have swept round the entire earth in twenty seven hours — moving at roughly the speed of sound.

Such an event would instantly destroy the uniformity principle.

Surprisingly, many scientists have attempted to fit this event into the accepted time scale, which was built up assuming the very theory which the event discredits.

More recent estimates put the diameter of the impacting body at between two hundred and four hundred kilometres. This would have produced a vastly bigger earthquake, vastly bigger tidal waves, and led to far more water being thrown up. Altogether the destruction of the uniformity idea would have been even more thorough.

This idea of a major blow to the earth's equilibrium is actually not new. More than half a century ago the famous Australian astronomer George Dodwell came to the conclusion that the earth has been disturbed from its original orientation by examining ancient measurements of the tilt of the earth's axis. The measurements show that the tilt has not followed the curve which most

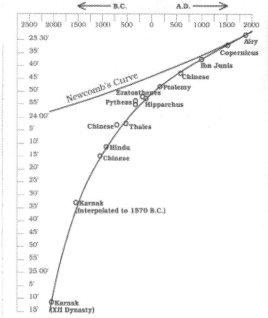

Illustration 15

Some of the observational values plotted by George Dodwell.
All the observations lie on a smooth curve, but do not correspond with Newcomb's theoretical curve. Newcomb assumed that the tilt of the axis was due only to the gravitational pull of the sun, moon and planets on the Earth's equatorial bulge. Dodwell came to suspect that Newcomb failed to take something important into account.

scientists assume it ought to have followed. The accepted curve, given by Stockwell's or Newcomb's formulae, assumes that the axis tilt depends on the gravitational pull of the sun, the moon and the planets acting on the earth's equatorial "bulge". But actual observations show that the reality is different. The observed and theoretical curves meet in about 1850, but prior to that date they diverge drastically. Dodwell analysed the difference between the observations and the theory, and came to the conclusion that the observations show a "logarithmic sine" curve, which is the curve of recovery of a top or gyroscope which has been disturbed from equilibrium by a blow. The curve becomes very steep before 2000 B.C., suggesting a major disturbing force acting somewhere in the region of five thousand years ago.

Such an idea is so contrary to the accepted views of science that Dodwell searched for confirmation in several different ways. Firstly he checked the accuracy of the observations of the ancient scientists. This is not difficult to do. The observations consist of measurements of the lengths of the shadows of a Gnomon (in principle just a vertical pillar standing on a level piece of ground) at the summer and winter solstices. The shadow lengths are used for calculating the tilt of the earth's axis. The same measurements can be used to calculate the latitude of the observing station. Dodwell thus had a check to see how accurate the measurements were. He simply used the measurements to predict the latitude of the observer, and compared that prediction with the known latitude. He accepted only values which checked to better than five

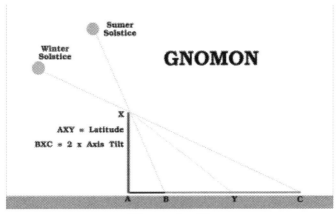

Illustration 16

In principle the Gnomon is simply a vertical pole standing on a level plane. The length of the shadow is measured at noon at midsummer and midwinter. The shadow lengths give the tilt of the Earth's axis, and also the latitude of the observer.

minutes of arc. Some were better than one minute of arc, which means that the shadow measurements effectively predict the observer's position on the surface of the Earth to considerably better than two kilometres.

The observers themselves had confidence in the accuracy of their measurements. The Roman mathematician Menilius, for example, after thirty years of observing the shadow of the great obelisk in Rome noted:- "… some change in the universal Earth, by which it has moved away from its centre, as I have detected myself, and hear of also in other places".

For a scientist to accept his observations rather than his preconceived ideas is not common, and shows confidence in the accuracy of his work. For comparison we could look at the record of the last hundred years. There are many examples of scientists believing their preconceived ideas rather than the observed data. One example is given by the measurements of the speed of light. Throughout the early part of the 20th century the measurements of the speed of light were consistently recorded as decreasing. Commenting on this M.E.J. Gheury de Bray said[22] :- "Invariably new determinations give values which are lower than the last one obtained, … there are twenty-two coincidences in favour of a decrease of the velocity of light, while there is not a single one against it". But so unwilling were scientists to accept the possibility of change in something that they had convinced themselves should be constant that the observations were considered incorrect, or in some way invalid. In fact, to get over the problem once and for all (hopefully!) the speed of light has now been defined as constant. This means that the metre is now a derived unit, and

Year of Measurement	Speed (km/sec)
1879	299 910 ± 50
1882	299 853 ± 60
1924	299 802 ± 30
1926	299 796 ± 4

Michelson's values for the speed of light. Other experimenters also found the same trend.

---

22   de Bray M.E.J.Gheury, *The Velocity of Light*, NATURE, 127, 522, April 4, 1931.

possibly subject to change, whereas speed, which used to be defined in terms of metres per second, has become underived and unchanging.[23]

But Menilius and his fellow scientists, had such confidence in the precision of their measurements that they were prepared to abandon their preconceived ideas of the constancy of the Earth and the Universe. This is strong testimony to their accuracy.

Dodwell then looked at ancient sun and star temples, and noticed an interesting pattern. Archaeologists examining such sites deduced dates for their construction based on historical considerations. About a hundred years ago, however, it became fashionable for astronomers to consider such temples, and they invariably found themselves at odds with the archaeologists. They deduced ages for the temples by using Newcomb's formula to determine when the sun and stars should have been in the required alignment. The ages they deduced were always far greater than those of the Archaeologists. At Stone-

Illustration 17
Archaeologists dated the construction of Stonehenge between 300 BC and 400 BC. Newcombe's theoretical curve suggests 1900 BC, but Dodwell's curve of observations points to 400 BC — in good agreement with archaeology.

23   For detailed discussion see *The Atomic Constants, Light and Time.*. Invited Research Report, Stanford Research International, and also Trioitsky V.S., ASTROPHYSICS AND SPACE SCIENCE, 139 (1987), pp.389-411.

henge in England, for example, the Archaeologists firmly concluded that the structure had been erected by the Druids between 300 and 400 B.C. Astronomers calculated that the alignment would only be correct in about 1900 B.C. The archaeologists were adamant, it was impossible, on several counts, that it could be so old. If Newcomb's formula were correct then it would have to be that old. But according to Dodwell's curve of observations, the alignment was correct in 400 B.C. — just when the archaeologists had deduced it must have been built. This suggests that the curve of observations is correct, whereas Newcomb's theoretical curve is not.

The most spectacular of all the ancient temples is the great temple of Ammon Ra at Karnak in Egypt. The archaeologists have sound reasons for believing their conclusions concerning the Karnak Temple: the pillars are covered with hieroglyphics describing its use and history. The inner sanctuary was used once each year, at sunset on the day of the summer solstice — the day of the year on which the sun rose highest in the sky, and was at its furthest north on the horizon at sunset. The temple was constructed so that at sunset on that day the sun was able to shine down a long avenue of sphinxes, between several sets of closely spaced pillars or "pylons", through the door of the sanctuary,

Illustration 18

The great temple of Ammon Ra (the Egyptian sun-god), the largest temple ever built. Although it is in ruins the plan is still clear.

across the altar and onto the golden statue of the sun god at the back. As the sun reached the horizon the doors were opened, pharaoh entered, bathed in sunlight, the sacrifice was offered on the altar, while the sun god shone magnificently in the rays of the setting sun.

The temple was constructed in stages, the last stage being completed by Ramses III in 1570 BC. The inscriptions on the columns state quite clearly that the sun shone into the sanctuary, with Ramses III entering like the sun god incarnate bathed in the sun's rays, and with the golden idol shining gloriously. But according to Newcomb's formula the sun could not have entered the sanctuary at that time. According to the accepted wisdom of Astronomy, the alignment of Karnak would only have been correct thousands of years earlier, on the previous cycle of Stockwell's curve. Dodwell's curve of observations

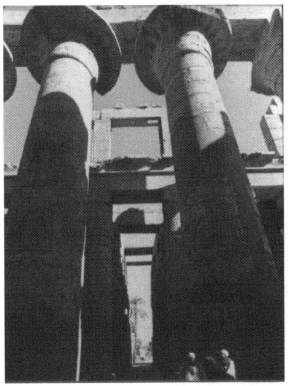

Illustration 19

Pylons at Karnak

Part of the central passage still stands. At the summer solstice the sun set far enough North along the horizon to shine through a long avenue of sphinxes, then through these pylons, through several more, and into the inner sanctuary. The final section was built by Ramses III in 1570 B.C. According to Newcombe's curve the sun could only have reached the altar many thousands of years earlier. According to Dodwell's curve of observations the sun would have entered at exactly the right date.

shows the sun at the correct alignment at exactly the right time, 1570 B.C.; Dodwell's conclusion:- the curve of observations is correct — Newcombe's theoretical curve is wrong.

Many other temples showed exactly the same situation. The alignments of the sun or stars to which the temples were erected fitted Dodwell's curve of observations at the time the archaeologists said they must have been built, but only corresponded with Newcomb's curve, as used by the astronomers, much earlier.

Dodwell became convinced that the curve of observations was correct, and that Newcomb's formula and Stockwell's formula had not taken into account something very significant. He concluded that the earth had received a great blow which disturbed its equilibrium less than 5 000 years ago. The impact of a meteorite of about 200 km diameter would fit the size of blow required to

Illustration 20

Hieroglyphics at Karnak

An archaeologist traces inscriptions at Karnak.

Hieroglyphics on the columns tell the story of the Karnak temple. We know when it was built, who built it, and how it was used.

account for the observations. That agrees well with the latest estimates coming from NASA.

The significant difference between the conclusions of Dodwell's investigation and the picture now becoming popular among the world's scientists is that Dodwell deduced the catastrophic event to have taken place less than five thousand years ago, whereas most scientists fit it into the geological

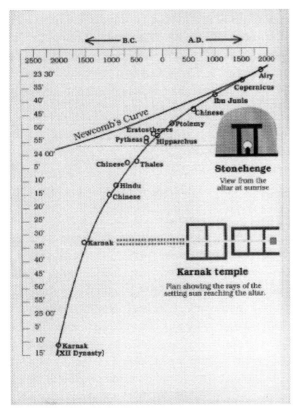

Illustration 21

Dodwell's curve with Stonehenge and Karnak

Astronomers used Newcombe's curve to determine that on the day of the Druids' dawn sacrifice at Stonehenge the sun would rise exactly over the "heelstone" (when seen from the altar) in 1900 B.C. Archeologists had dated the construction between 300 BC and 400 BC. Dodwell's curve of observations shows that the alignment wouldhave been correct in 400 B.C., in very good agreement with Archaeology.

Newcombe's curve predicts that the alignment of the great temple at Karnak could not have been correct. At the summer solstice the setting sun could not have shone down the avenue of sphinxes, between the pylons and onto the altar in the inner sanctuary. Dodwell's curve of observations shows that the alignment was indeed correct when Ramses III finished the construction in 1570 B.C.

Hieroglyphics on the columns assure us that the setting sun did shine onto the altar when the temple was completed.

Dodwell concluded that the observations are correct, whereas Newcombe's theory had neglected to consider some important factor.

column at sixty-five million years ago, even though the event itself would have destroyed the very basis on which Lyell and his disciples built this time scale.

The devastating nature of such an event is hard to imagine. Tidal waves of even fifteen metres are fearsome agents of destruction. Waves several kilo-metres high, travelling at the speed of sound, and sweeping round the entire earth in twenty seven hours are totally unknown today Their power can only be guessed at. The effect of hundreds of millions of millions of tons of water, and hundreds of millions of millions of tons of steam being thrown up into the atmosphere with the power of a multi-million-megaton explosion is again totally out of the realm of our experience. The effect of a global earthquake, millions of times more powerful than those now experienced, can also only be speculated upon.

But obviously these events, all occurring simultaneously, would cause a vast amount of geological work to be accomplished very quickly. The fact that from the Cambrian period to the Recent no meteorites have been found leads to the question of whether a major part of that section of the column might have been laid down rapidly as a result of such a catastrophe.

Although this idea is not popular today, most geologists of the pre-Lyellian era believed that the majority of the sedimentary rocks of the earth had, in-deed, been laid down in one watery catastrophe. The vast majority of the sedimentary rocks have the appearance of having been laid down continu-ously and rapidly in water. But some features of the rock strata do not seem to fit in with that idea. For example, there are surfaces at some levels in the strata where it appears that clay has been exposed to the air, under such con-ditions that it dried out and cracked. There are sediments which appear to have been laid down in very shallow water, and there are even surfaces which appear to consist of heaps of wind-blown sand. It has been asked how such features could have occurred if the entire earth were experiencing a cata-strophic flood.

It is, of course, not possible to say how such features formed, we have no eye-witness report of what happened. But we do have eye-witness reports of very much smaller events which have happened in more recent times.

For example, on 18th August 1868 the U.S.S. Wateree, a flat-bottomed paddle steamer, was anchored in the harbour of Arica, which was then in Peru (it is now in Chile). An earthquake struck the town and levelled it to the ground.

An hour later the first tidal wave generated by the earthquake engulfed the survivors in the town, and then receded, leaving the Wateree upright on the bottom, and leaving other ships, which did not have flat bottoms, on their beam ends, high and dry.

Lieutenant Billings, one of the officers of the Wateree, reported that the sun had set when the lookout spotted the next wave. "We made out a thin phosphorescent line ... rising higher and higher." Below it loomed "frightful masses of black water". The fifty foot (fifteen metre) high tidal wave swallowed the Wateree and deposited it at the foot of a mountain several kilometres away.

The first point to note concerning this report is that fifteen metre high waves are absolutely "frightful", very powerful and destructive — and as nothing compared to five kilometre high waves.

The second point to note is that the ships were left high and dry on the bottom.

For the water surface to rise in one place it must go down somewhere else.

The third point to note is that not all of the waves generated were of the same size — the second was the biggest and most powerful.

And finally the sea bed was left exposed for quite some time between waves.

Conditions following a major meteorite impact cannot really be known, but scientists have done calculations to gain some idea of what it might have been like. One of them, Edward Anders, a cosmochemist from the University of Chicago, describing the impact of a ten kilometre diameter body said:- "Even if it hit the ocean, the impact would have created a crater 300 kilometres across. A huge plume would have pushed the atmosphere aside. The fireball would have had a radius of several thousand kilometres. Winds of hundreds of kilometres an hour would have swept the planet for hours, drying trees like a giant hair drier."[24] This rather suggests that it is not impossible for beds of clay to have dried out to the point of cracking during the twenty hours or so that they may have lain exposed awaiting the arrival of the next wave with its vast quantities of sediment. Also since the hot dry winds had "fireball" temperatures and immense speeds, and behaved like "giant hair driers" they might have dried out a considerable amount of sand and blown it into heaps.

---

24 Anders E. quoted in National Geographic, June 1989, p.673.

Another feature found in the geological record which has often been held to refute the possibility that it could have formed very quickly is the presence of striations (scratches) and unsorted deposits called tills (in which clay, sand and boulders are all dumped together). It has been said that these must be evidence for ice having covered large areas of the globe for long periods of time. Rocks carried along by ice can scratch the rock over which the ice is moving. When ice melts it drops everything it is carrying, coarse or fine, all at once. Since ice moves very slowly it must have taken vast amounts of time to leave such features. But it has been discovered fairly recently that earthquakes cause mud-flows, chiefly under the sea, but also on land. Mud flows can carry rocks which make striations. They also dump unsorted tills. Mudflows cause features so like those produced by ice that even experts are hardput to tell which agent was responsible[25]. Mud flows have been measured to travel at over a hundred kilometres per hour, whereas ice travels at centimetres per year. Until fairly recently no agent other than ice was known which

Illustration 22

The eruption of Mount St. Helens in 1980 caused both rapid deposition and rapid erosion. These sediments were laid down in a matter of hours, but show all the features which uniformitarian geology would interpret as requiring vast ages of time. (Photo: Steve Austin)

25 Dott R., *Tilite or Sub-aqueous Slide*, program Abstracts, Geological Soc. of America, 1959.

could cause these features. We now know that mud can also, but there may be other processes, perhaps as yet unobserved, which are also able to cause the same features. Huge mud-flows would certainly have accompanied the kind of impact that many scientists now claim did take place — it seems that long ice ages may not have been needed to form such features in the record of the rocks. Evidence for recent glaciation lasting several hundred years is not in doubt. Only interpretation of the geological record is here questioned.

Varves are another feature which were believed to represent evidence for great age until very recently. Varved rock has alternate bands of coarse and fine material. For many years it was believed, usually stated as fact, that the coarse layer was a result of rapid inflow of water in summer, whereas the fine layer represented the slow settling of fine clay during winter. Thus each alternation of coarse and fine material was believed to represent one year. Some varved beds contain thousands of layers, hence the beds were seen to be the result of thousands of years of deposition. But when scientists actually got down to being scientific about the matter and made observations, it was discovered that several layers could be observed to form in one year. A French-

Illustration 23

Varved Rock

Alternate bands of coarse and fine material called "varves". For many years it was assumed that one coarse and one fine layer formed each year.

man, Guy Berthault, then performed some experiments in which he poured a mixture of coarse and fine material through water and discovered that varves form by re-arrangement of material already deposited, apparently drawing the energy required from the material striking the surface above them. He produced hundreds of such layers in a very short time. When he ground up varved rock and re-deposited through water he found the same thicknesses of coarse and fine layers as in the original rock.[26]

26   Berthault G., COMPTES RENDUS, Acad.Sc.Paris, t.303, Serie II. no.17, 1986, pp1569-1574. English translation in C.E.N. Technical Journal Vol.3 (1988) pp.25-29.

One of the most significant points to note about this is that for many years varves were put forward as proof that the rock record represents vast amounts of time. It has come to light that this is not so. It is not unreasonable to suspect that similar claims for other phenomena may be on an equally poor foundation. This certainly appears to be the case for erosion features like the Grand Canyon. For many years it was claimed that the Grand Canyon had been cut out by the Colorado River, which at present erodes material so slowly that it would have taken several million years to produce the Canyon. In 1980 the Mount St. Helens eruption was accompanied by an earthquake which produced mud flows which excavated a major canyon system, Engineer's Canyon, in a very short time. This canyon now contains the north fork of the Toutle River, but the river did not carve out the canyon, the river is simply there because another cause produced a feature which is essentially a drainage system. What reason is there then to believe that the Grand Canyon was not also excavated by a similar mechanism, or even by a completely different, perhaps as yet unidentified, mechanism? Many features of the Canyon are totally inconsistent with the idea that the Colorado River produced it. Many features appear to be those of rapid gully erosion. Experiments which have attempted to duplicate the incised meanders (meanders cut through many layers of rock), show that they can only be formed when all of the layers are soft. If any layers are hard, then the river cuts sideways instead of downwards and the meander pattern is destroyed. If all the layers had to be soft then it is possible that they were laid down in rapid succession and eroded quickly by run-off water before any layer had the opportunity to dry out and become hard.

Illustration 24

Engineer's Canyon, a major drainage system in which flows the North fork of the Toutle River. The canyon was carved out in one day by a mud flow accompanying the St. Helen's eruption in 1980. (Photo: Steve Austin)

It is more difficult than might at first be imagined to find really convincing hard evidence that conflicts with Dodwell's proposal that a major catastrophe, which completely changed the face of the earth, happened in the region of five thousand years ago. Reliable written records do not go any further back in history than five thousand years. The time scale of the anthropologists is based on evolutionary speculation. Radiocarbon dating has been shown to be unreliable (its unreliability increases markedly with the age of the specimen being dated). Even tree ring dating is not perfectly reliable. Deciduous trees produce a pattern of rings, each of which usually represents one year's growth. Counting the rings is a fairly reliable means of finding the age of a deciduous tree. But the really old trees are evergreens which do not seasonally lose their leaves. Their rings (less distinct, and often difficult to make out) represent alternating periods of slow and rapid growth. This may represent rapid growth in summer and slow growth in winter, but it may also represent slow growth during a period of insect attack, rapid growth during an unusually warm, wet winter, etc. Evergreens can produce more than one ring per year and therefore may be untrustworthy for establishing chronology. Tree ring chronologies which have been put together from living and long dead tree remains are less trustworthy still; they rely on radiocarbon dating (which is notoriously unreliable) and on matching similar patterns of rings, which may also be prone to error.

There is evidence that the earth's atmosphere used to be denser than at present. A number of very large flying reptiles, pterosaurs, seem aerodynamically unsuited to the present atmosphere - it is hard to see how they could have flown at all. Somewhat smaller flying reptile could apparently have flown if they had been able to launch themselves from a height, but could not have become airborne otherwise. With double the atmospheric pressure they could have flown normally. Plants seem to have been designed for about twice the present atmospheric pressure. Transpiration rates at present atmospheric pressure are far higher than needed, and lead to a serious problem. Often plants suffer because they have profligately transpired away the available water at a far higher rate than needed. At twice the pressure they transpire very efficiently. This is strange when compared to the efficiency with which plants utilise sunlight. They seem to have been designed for exactly the light available. Ahrens and O'Keef's calculations show a ten kilometre bolide having the power of a thousand million megaton bomb, throwing ten million-million tons of water and a similar quantity of steam up at enormous speed. It is possible that such an event could have blasted off a considerable part of the original atmosphere into space. If the evolutionary scenario were true, and the event happened sixty five million years ago, then plants should have had time for evolutionary change to regain efficiency in transpiration. If it happened only a few thousand years ago though, we could expect what we actually find.

As a final point there is an interesting archaeological site, Tiahuanaco near Lake Titicaca in South America. Archaeologists working on Tiahuanaco say that it was constructed about four thousand years ago. There is evidence that it was built at sea level. It was, apparently, a seaside town. It had a large population, huge grain stores and large markets. It is now four thousand metres above sea level. It is so high and so cold that it is completely deserted, visited in summer by a few shepherds who bring their sheep up to graze on the hardy grasses which manage to survive the brief growing season. Within a few thousand years it appears to have changed from being a seaside town in a rich agricultural area, to a mountain ruin four thousand metres above sea level.

At the end of the Louisiana conference Professor Kasman looked at the evidence and summed up like this:- "cosmochronology and geochronology are far from reliable in yielding ages ... therefore ... many engineering structures or designs that were based on such determinations, whether for the containment of radio-active waste or evaluation of activities of faults would be questionable if not downright hazardous!"

Most of the ideas of speculative science seem to have little immediate effect on our daily life. What matter if the universe began fifteen thousand million years ago in a primordial explosion or not? What matter if the stars produce their light and heat by thermonuclear reactions or not? There are, actually, very major philosophical, religious and moral implications. But in the question of the history of the earth, if the speculations of popular science are wrong then the direct physical consequences could be drastic for people of all philosophies, all religious persuasions, and all codes of moral behaviour. The consequences could be, as Kasman put it, "downright hazardous".

And there certainly seem to be plenty of reasons for believing that the popular speculations are very wrong indeed. Whether a meteorite impact (or a series of such impacts) is the reason or part of the reason, or not even a reality at all is not actually the point at issue. The question is what really is the time scale?

And that raises the question, leading of necessity to much deeper issues: How long have we actually been here?

Chapter 4

How On Earth Did We Get Here?

As far as most questions open to speculation are concerned, man has proved himself very ingenious and creative in his speculations. Before accurate measurements were able to establish that the earth is globular many ideas were put forward regarding its shape and form. Some had the earth flat — circular or rectangular — some had it supported on columns or pillars or on the backs of giant elephants or turtles or floating on a great ocean. But as far as the question of how life, and man in particular, came to be here, there have been amazingly few possibilities offered for consideration.

In fact there seem to be precisely two rival explanations, no more.

Currently the one more favoured by the media is evolution — life came about by naturalistic processes, by pure chance, and gradually progressed from simple to complex. The other alternative is that life was created in much the form we see it now by an external creator. That these two seem to be the only alternatives was forcefully pointed out by Sir Arthur Keith when he said[1] "Evolution is unproven and unprovable, we believe it because the only alternative is special creation."

If the impression given by the media is correct, it seems that the majority of scientists today support the idea of evolution. Even though it remains "unproven and unprovable", evolution has been the central idea of almost the whole of science for about a hundred and fifty years. In view of which it is rather surprising that when Dr. Colin Patterson, senior palaeontologist of the British Museum, gave his keynote address at a conference in the American Museum of Natural History in November 1981, he presented a rather strange

---

1 Keith Sir Arthur, quoted in DID MAN JUST HAPPEN?, p. 46

question to the assembled evolution specialists. The question was "Can you tell me anything you know about evolution, any one thing, any one thing that is true?" He had asked that question at other seminars in America and the only answer he got was silence. At the Evolutionary Morphology Seminar at the University of Chicago the answer was a long silence until someone eventually said, "I do know one thing — it ought not to be taught in high school".

For many years the biologists and palaeontologists have approached their observations and their data with the question "How can the observations be fitted into the theory of evolution?" By devising suitable ad hocs, and by ignoring certain hard-to-explain data, it has usually been possible to fit most of the observations very plausibly into the theory.

It is certainly possible to put forward a very convincing case for several aspects of the theory. But in view of the response to Patterson's question perhaps it would be wise to consider another question:- "Is evolution possible at all?"

First we need to notice that the theory of evolution as told to the common public divides itself naturally into two parts. In the first part non-living matter comes together (by purely random chance processes) to form some kind of living organism, some "simple" single celled life form like a bacterium or amoeba. Although no trace has ever been found of an arguably "living" form simpler than a bacterium, many biologists have speculated that something simpler might once have existed, in which case the appearance of this "protobacterium" would be the first stage. The second part of the theory requires that further random chance accidental processes bring changes to this organism, changes which lead to progress, development, and increasing complexity. It is a fundamental requirement for both phases of the theory that there is no intelligence involved in the process, no design, no goal, simply random statistical natural processes which proceed entirely by themselves. The second phase is different from the first in one important detail. Once the process of reproduction has evolved, natural selection is presumed to lead to disadvantageous changes being eliminated and advantageous ones being preserved because the advantaged creatures will be more likely to produce a greater number of offspring.

The first stage of this process, the evolution of life from non-life, received a boost in 1953 when Stanley Miller performed a famous experiment in which he put some chemicals, particularly ammonia and methane, together with hydrogen and water vapour, into an apparatus and bombarded them with high energy radiation. [2] He discovered that in the tarry sludge produced, a small proportion of the chemicals were organic compounds similar to those used by living organisms. This was trumpeted by the media as if he had produced life in a test-tube. That is actually very far from the truth; he had simply produced some interesting chemicals including amino acids, which are the building blocks from which proteins are made.

Similar experiments were performed by other scientists in laboratories all over the world. It was discovered that there are several difficulties for the idea that this could be the first stage in the evolution of life from non-life.

Firstly only "racemic mixtures" of left-handed and right-handed amino acids could be produced. All known life forms can only use left-handed amino acids for their proteins; one right-handed amino acid renders a protein useless. It has been found possible to filter them, but it seems somewhat far-fetched to imagine that a suitable filter would be available just at the right time, just by chance.

Secondly, proteins are made of twenty different kinds of amino acid. Not all of those required have been produced by this kind of experiment and even those which are produced are in very low concentrations.

Another difficulty is that a trap has to be used to extract the amino acids immediately after formation, because otherwise the high energy radiation destroys them as quickly as they are produced. It seems somewhat far-fetched to imagine that a suitable trap would be available just by chance.

The next difficulty is that unless there is free hydrogen in the mixture no amino acids form. Also if there is the slightest trace of oxygen in the mixture no amino acids form. It was proposed (in fact, put forward as proven.), that the earth did, indeed, have such an atmosphere at some stage. But it has now been established that if there ever was such an atmosphere, it must have been for such a short time, and in such unfavourable circumstances, that it could not possibly have been of any use in any process of evolution.

The next problem is that examination of "ancient sea beds" has not revealed the slightest trace of the amino acid-rich "prebiotic soup" that the theory requires. The soup remains purely unsubstantiated speculation with the observations stacked heavily against it.

---

2   Miller S.L., *Production of Amino Acids Under Possible Primitive Earth Conditions*, SCIENCE, Vol 117, 1953, p. 528.

Perhaps the biggest problem of all is the fact that the earth has always had plenty of free water. The kind of chemical reactions involved always go "the wrong way" in the presence of excess water. Instead of building up to more complex forms, when water is abundantly present they break down into simpler forms. In chemical terms they are of the kind:- $A + B \longrightarrow C + H_2O$. In the presence of free water what actually happens is $C + H_2O \longrightarrow A + B$

Although the idea of life on earth beginning in an ocean of "prebiotic soup" is still widely taught in schools and promoted in museums and popular magazines, such problems soon convinced the evolutionists involved that life must have started in some other way.

A number of ideas on this were proposed. One of the most notable is that put forward by Francis Crick, a scientist who rose to fame when he gained a Nobel prize for his part in deciphering the genetic code. His idea is fairly typical. In his book "Life Itself"[3], Crick speculated that life must have originated on some far distant planet. Speculations like this assume that on such a planet an atmosphere of methane, ammonia, hydrogen, etc. actually did exist. Also there must have been no oxygen and little water. High energy radiation produced amino acids, random chance processes filtered out the left-handed from the right-handed. The left-handed came together to form proteins which assembled themselves into a living organism. This organism multiplied and eventually transformed the methane, ammonia and hydrogen into an oxygen rich atmosphere (producing abundant water in the process), so that higher life could develop. Evolution proceeded until a very advanced civilization came into being. Eventually the members of this civilization put genetic material into some kind of space vehicle, which eventually reached planet Earth.

More recently scientists have been speculating on an alternative possibility. A world full of complex structures called RNA might have brought forth the first life, Experts in this theory have described it as a "Molecular Biologist's Dream", in which "… it is assumed that a magic catalyst existed to convert the activated nucleotides to a random ensemble of polynucleotide sequences, a subset of which had the ability to replicate".[4]

Mendeleev pointed out that measurement is the starting point of science. Albert Einstein said that what can be measured is science, everything else is specu-

---

3   Crick F., LIFE ITSELF, Macdonald & Co., London & Sydney, 1982.

4   Gesteland R.F and Atkins J.F. (editors), THE RNA WORLD, Cold Spring Harbour Laboratory Press, 1993, p. 7.

lation. The far distant planet hypothesis sounds much more like speculation than science. And what can one say of the molecular biologist's dream of magic catalysts in an RNA World? If we want to get to a scientific perspective we have to move to the realm of measurement, to the realm of numbers, mathematics.

The kind of numbers needed are very large ones. For those unfamiliar with such numbers it will be useful to take a quick look at powers of ten. "Ten to the power two" (written 10^2) means one with two noughts after it, in other words one hundred. "Ten to the power six" (written 10^6) means one with six noughts after it, in other words one million. Consider as a basic unit one millimetre. One kilometre is a million (10^6) millimetres. The diameter of the earth is 12 740 km, roughly 10^{10}mm. The number of millimetres to the moon is between 10^{11} and 10^{12}.

The number of millimetres to the sun is about 10^{14}. Now we are in the realm of large numbers. Beyond the solar system astronomical distances are very speculative, they are based on unverified assumptions, and are therefore not reliable. But if we accept the distances popularly believed, then we find that:- The number of millimetres to the nearby stars is somewhat less than 10^{20}.

The far distant galaxies, which can only be seen with powerful telescopes are thought to be about 10^{30}mm. away.

So 10^{30} is an astronomically large number — it is almost impossible to imagine all those millimetres stretching off into the distance. It would take a beam

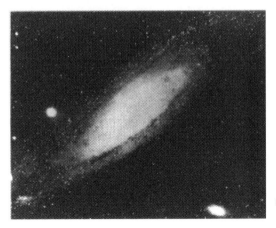

Illustration 25

Andromeda Galaxy

The Andromeda Galaxy is popularly believed to be so far away that light travelling at 300 000 km/sec would take two million years to reach us. If that is true, then its distance from the Earth is about ten to the power twenty-five millimetres   (1 followed by 25 zeros)

of light (travelling at 300 000 km. every second) more than ten thousand million years to cover that distance.

We can see why Emil Borel, who is a probability expert, said[5] :- "Odds beyond one in 10^{50} have a zero probability of ever happening, and even that gives it the benefit of the doubt".

10^{50} is an unimaginably huge number. If every one of the millimetres to the far distant galaxies were expanded to the distance from here to the stars we would have 10^{50} millimetres. One chance in 10^{50} is the chance of picking out a particular one of all those millimetres at the first try, blindfold. It is about the same chance as a punter buying one ticket for a national or state lottery every week for a month and winning every time. Such a thing has never happened, and if it did ever happen nobody would doubt that there was cheating going on. It seems reasonable to accept what Borel says, one chance in 10^{50} means no chance at all, no possibility at all of it ever happening purely by accident.

Most evolutionists are biologists, palaeontologists, or specialists in related fields. They usually have very little liking for mathematics. For such scientists these huge numbers usually seem to have some sort of a magical quality about them. This "magical" attribute of large numbers can be seen in a statement made by professor George Wald, one of the most famous evolutionary professors of the 20th century. He said[6] :- "The time with which we have to deal is of the order of two billion years. What we regard as impossible on the basis of human experience is meaningless here. Given so much time, the 'impossible' becomes possible, the possible probable, and the probable virtually certain. One only has to wait, time itself performs the miracles".

To such scientists there is something miraculous about these huge numbers. Perhaps the most miraculous idea of all was that put forward by Thomas Huxley in the original evolution debate. In this story he proposed a monkey sitting at a typewriter hitting keys at random. Eventually, if it types for long enough, just by chance, just by random accident, it will type out the works of William Shakespeare. This may be the most powerful argument ever put forward for the theory of evolution, it demonstrates that unlikely events can happen if given sufficient time. Time, apparently, can perform miracles if there is enough of it.

---

5 Borel E., ELEMENTS OF THE THEORY OF PROBABILITY, Prentice Hall.

6 Wald G., *The Origin of Life*, SCIENTIFIC AMERICAN, Vol.191(2), August 1954, p. 48.

But is there enough of it?

What happens if we actually put some numbers into the idea? Consider just the first line of the first page, the title:-

"The Complete Works of William Shakespeare".

What is the chance of typing out just that first line by pure chance? On the typewriter section of the keyboard that this book was typed on, the likelihood of doing it by accident is one chance in 10^{76}. Not all typewriters have exactly the same arrangement of keys, so another keyboard may give another value — but not very much different.

One chance in 10^{76}; what does that look like in terms of our monkeys?

The longest estimate for the age of the universe according to the popular "Big Bang" theory is twenty thousand million (20 x 10^9) years. That is 6.3 x 10^{17} seconds.

To give any chance of writing out that first line we would need ($10^{76}/ 6.3 \times 10^{17}$) = 1.6 x 10^{58} monkeys each hitting one key every second for all that time!

Each monkey has about 10^{30} elementary particles (protons, neutrons and electrons). So the number of particles needed for all the monkeys is 1.6 x 10^{88}.

But it is believed that the total number of particles in the entire visible universe is less than 10^{80}. So we need more than a hundred million times more monkeys than can be made from all the material in the universe, and there is nothing left to make their typewriters with.

Huxley's idea of monkeys typing out Shakespeare does not seem quite so convincing any more.

If we had accepted what Borel had said in the first place, we would have had no need to do the calculations. One chance in 10^{76} is much less than one chance in 10^{50}. So we could have seen immediately that there is no possibility that this can happen just by accident. That line was obviously typed out deliberately, not by chance. As soon as one starts to put numbers into the probabilities involved with evolution, it becomes clear that there is something very wrong. Mathematicians, engineers and physicists pointed out that evolution has a major credibility problem. So a symposium was called, a famous symposium at the Wistar Institute in America. Some of the world's top scientists were there.

The symposium was called "Mathematical Challenges to the Neo-Darwinian Interpretation of Evolution". The first technical paper was presented by Professor Murray Eden, professor of Engineering at Massachusetts Institute of Technology. One of the first things he did was to point out that the probability of assembling a typical biological protein by random processes (from an adequate supply of all the necessary amino acids) is one chance in 10^{325}.[7] Now that is unimaginably smaller than the probability of our monkeys typing out the Shakespearean title. The probability of this happening by chance on Borel's estimation is a very great deal less than no chance at all. We are now at the stage where our hopeful punter buys one state lottery ticket each week for six months and wins every single time. Even the most optimistic daydreamer in the world knows it is not going to happen - at least, not by chance.

Proteins are long strings of twenty different kinds of amino acid in a very specific sequence folded to a precise shape. Enzymes are a very important class of proteins. Each enzyme has what is called an "active site", a specially shaped key, which has to fit what is called a "substrate" (for example glucose), like a key in a lock. The fit has to be perfect. It has to be correct to one atom. Because of the limitations on the active site of enzymes, because they have to be so exact, it is possible to do statistical analyses to see how possible it would be to produce enzymes by chance. The simplest known living organism has more than two hundred thousand individual proteins, and of those more than two thousand are enzymes. Just to produce those two thousand enzymes (from a copious supply of all the required amino acids) the probability is one chance in $10^{40\,000}$, a number so large that to write it out by hand takes about twenty pages.[8] Even if the probabilities of combination for the various types of amino acid are not all the same, and even if their combination might be a process which can "remember" what happened in the past, leading to enormous acceleration of later stages, analysis shows that at most one thousand of the forty thousand zeros could be removed, reducing the improbability to one chance in $10^{39\,000}$. That is about the probability of someone buying one lottery ticket every week for fifty four years and winning every single time.

And this is only the start of the problem for evolution.

---

7   Eden M., MATHEMATICAL CHALLENGES TO THE NEO-DARWINIAN INTERPRETATION OF EVOLUTION, The Wistar Institute of Anatomy and Biology, 1966, Ed. Paul S. Moorhead & Martin M. Kaplan, p. 7.

8   Hoyle Sir Fred, THE INTELLIGENT UNIVERSE, p. 17.

Illustration 27
Ribosome
Messenger RNA carrying coded Information enters the ribosome which reads a block of code (called a codon). The code determines which amino acid is specified. The ribosome calls a transfer RNA carrying the correct amino acid.

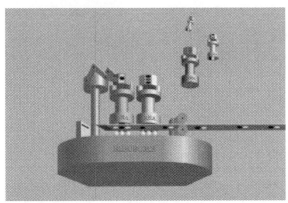

The messenger RNA is moved forward one codon, the second block of code is read and the specified tRNA called into place. The first amino acid is checked, and if correct, taken from the first tRNA and chained onto the second amino acid.

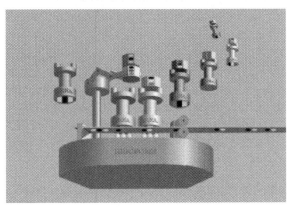

The messenger RNA moves forward another codon, the first tRNA is now free to go and collect another amino acid. Meanwhile, the third block of code is read, and the correct tRNA called into place. The second amino acid is checked, and if correct it (together with the first, which is now joined to it) is chained onto the third amino acid.

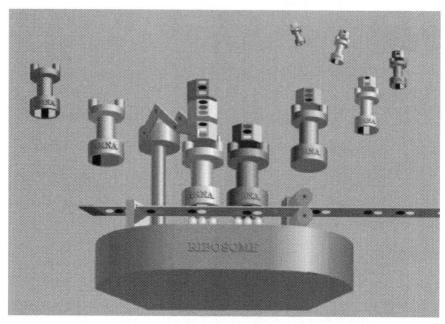

Illustration 27
Ribosome (continued)

The process continues with the mRNA moving forward one codon at a time, specified amino acids being called into place, and the growing chain being added until the entire protein is complete. The accuracy with which the ribosome of the simplest bacterium builds proteins surpasses the copying accuracy of the world's best computers. The amount and critical complexity of the information handled means that lesser accuracy would rapidly lead to error catastrophe and extinction.

The simplest known living organism has an apparatus called a "ribosome". The ribosome of the simplest known living organism is as complex and as accurate as that possessed by man. A ribosome is an amazing piece of apparatus. It has a kind of reading mechanism analogous to that of a tape recorder. The ribosome moves along a thread of messenger RNA (mRNA), which is a working copy of a section of the genetic code stored in the DNA of an organism. The first part of the head reads the code of one unit of information called a "codon".

It deciphers the code, decides what amino acid is specified and summons a transfer-RNA (tRNA) molecule which carries that particular amino acid. When a tRNA with the correct amino acid arrives, the mRNA is moved through the head to the next codon. This codon is deciphered, and the tRNA with the specified amino acid called in. The ribosome then takes the amino acid from the first tRNA and chains it onto that carried by the second. The first tRNA is now free to go and seek another amino acid of its specific kind. The mRNA is moved through the ribosome so that the third codon enters the reading head, the third tRNA is called into place, and the growing chain is taken from the second tRNA and added to the third's amino acid. This process is repeated, the growing chain being added each time to the newly summoned amino acid until the protein is complete. A typical protein has about two hundred and fifty amino acids; some proteins have thousands. When the whole process is finished the ribosome releases the string of amino acids and passes it to folding jigs which fold it to its characteristic, and very complex, form. The accuracy with which the ribosome works far surpasses the electronic computer — although modern computers make hardly any mistakes the ribosome makes far fewer. The complexity of the folded form is such that a Cray1 supercomputer takes months of continuous calculation to work out the required shape. The simplest bacterium folds many different kinds of proteins every second.

To calculate the probability that such a complex and accurate mechanism could make itself just by chance would be difficult, but it is obviously far less than the probability of simply producing the enzymes we considered earlier. But we are still hardly beginning to scratch the surface of the problem, because the simplest living organism has a thread of DNA, which is a marvel of information storage miniaturization. It is, in effect, a "computer program", of immense length and complexity, which specifies the proteins of life (see Illustration 28). The simplest known living organism has a thread of DNA containing information equivalent to hundreds of books full of complex information. The probability of producing that just by chance is absolutely mind-boggling. But for the creation of the simplest known living organism we must have all of these things (and many more) in existence at the same time. To calculate the probability of that happening just by chance is very difficult, but attempts have been made. "By adding up the energy content of all the chemical bonds in a 'simple' bacterium, and comparing this to the energy content at equilibrium of the constituent atoms from which it was formed, Morowitz calculated the probability of this cell to be ten to the minus one hundred thousand million".[9] In other words, the chance of just the physical structure of the simplest bacterium forming by chance is one chance in $10^{100\,000\,000\,000}$. Roughly the chance of our one ticket each week gambler winning the na-

9   Gish D.T., *A Consistent View on the Origin of Life*, C.S.R.Q. Vol. 15 No 4.

tional lottery every week for fourteen million years.

That is, of course, a very great deal less, unimaginably less, mind-bogglingly less, than no chance at all.

And that is only the probability of producing the physical structure on which the simplest known form of life can ride. [10]

One can see why the great scientist Professor Sir Fred Hoyle reacted to such analysis by saying:- "The notion that not only the biopolymers, but the operating program of a living cell could be arrived at by chance in a primordial soup here on the Earth is evidently nonsense of a high order".[11]

If the scientists can see that the idea of life arising by chance is nonsense of a high order, how is it possible to continue to believe in evolution?

This question was addressed at the Wistar symposium. The first explanation put forward was by Dr. Conway Zirkle; he said[12] :- "Now, what is the probability of any one of us being here in this room?"

This is a variant of a very popular argument. The argument has two forms, one of them does not actually make much sense, since it simply extends the improbability of a simple organism to one or more highly complex organisms. The variation which makes sense argues that there are thousands of millions of people in the world. There are millions of buildings in the world, many of them with many rooms. The chance of finding one particular person in one particular room is extremely small, and yet here we all are, in this room, the probability of it happening is infinitesimal, and yet it has happened — which shows that improbable events do, indeed, happen.

There is, however, a problem with that argument. The theory demands that evolution happens purely by chance. Just by accidental statistical processes. But not one of the people were in that room by accident. Every person there had received an invitation, thought about it, and having decided to go, had

---

10   It does not help to point out that there are simpler objects, like viruses, which do not have all these structures. Viruses are unable to reproduce by themselves, they have to invade a living organism and pirate the use of machinery like the ribosome.

11   Hoyle Sir Fred, NEW SCIENTIST, Vol 92, No. 1280

12   Zirkle C., MATHEMATICAL CHALLENGES ... , p. 19

taken deliberate steps to get to that room at that time. Not one of them was there by chance. In effect, what this argument says is that we have to bring in intelligence; every person in that room was there because of intelligent decisions.

A second explanation was put forward by a very famous evolutionist, Professor Sewal Wright. He said[13] :- "On the principle of the children's game of twenty questions, in which it is possible to arrive at the correct one of about a million objects by a succession of 20 yes-or-no answers, it would require less than 1250 questions to arrive at a specified one of these proteins".

But he runs into the same problem as Dr. Zirkle. The game of twenty questions only works because of intelligence. It takes a pretty reasonable intelligence (and a fair memory) to get the answer within twenty guesses. What is needed to play a game that requires one thousand two hundred and fifty questions to arrive at the answer? Again the problem can only be solved by intelligence — and apparently a very considerable intelligence.

A third solution has been put forward by an even more famous evolutionist, Professor George Gaylord Simpson. He said[14] :- "Suppose that from a pool of all the letters of the alphabet in large, equal abundance you tried to draw simultaneously the letters "C ", "A", "T", in order to achieve a purposeful combination of these into the word "CAT". Drawing out three letters at a time and then discarding them if they did not form this useful combination, you obviously would have very little chance of achieving your purpose .... But now suppose that every time you draw a "C", an "A", or a "T" in a wrong combination you are allowed to put these desirable letters back in the pool and to discard the undesirable letters. Now you are sure of obtaining your result, and your chances of obtaining it quickly are much improved."

The problem with this is that not only do we need intelligence — to decide whether an "R" or a "Y" for example are useful or not — we also need to know our goal. The theory of evolution demands that there is no plan, there is no design, there is no predetermined goal. But to know that an "R" is useless to our purpose whereas a "T" is essential, we have to know the final result (CAT) to which we are heading. Simpson had to abandon the basic principles of evolution as did his colleagues at the Wistar symposium.

---

13 Wright S., MATHEMATICAL CHALLENGES ... , p. 117

14 Simpson, G.G., *The Problem of Plan and Purpose in Nature*, SCIENTIFIC MONTHLY, 64: p. 493.

To get over the first step in evolution, the evolution of life from non-living matter, there seems to be no reasonable alternative but to abandon the basic principles of the theory.

But there is another possibility: to ignore the fact that it is "nonsense of a high order", and simply accept by faith that it did actually happen. It obviously requires a very great deal of faith to accept probabilities of the order of 1 chance in $10^{100\,000\,000\,000\,000}$. But it appears that some do, indeed, have such a strong faith.

Not all evolutionists acknowledge that evolution is, in fact, a faith, but it was clearly noted by Professor G. A. Kerkut[15] when he said:- "It is therefore a matter of faith on the part of the biologist that biogenesis did occur and he can choose whatever method of biogenesis happens to suit him personally; the evidence for what did happen is not available".

It is not only the first step of evolution which has to be held by faith, the second part of the story, the evolution of one life form into another is also held by faith. That the whole of evolution is a matter of faith was clearly recognized by another well-known evolutionist, Professor L. Harrison Matthews[16], when he said:- "The fact of evolution is the backbone of biology, and biology is thus in the peculiar position of being a science founded on an unproved theory — is it then a science or a faith? Belief in evolution is thus exactly parallel to belief in special creation — both are concepts which believers know to be true but neither, up to the present, has been capable of proof".

Since it is believed without any proof, it can hardly be considered to have anything to do with science. It has to do with religion. This was even more openly spelled out by Professor H.S. Lipson[17] when he said:- "In fact, evolution became in a sense a scientific religion; almost all scientists have accepted it and many are prepared to 'bend' their observations to fit in with it".

Another clear indication of the religious implications was given by Julian Huxley, one of the most influential evolutionists of all time. On an American

15 Kerkut, G.A., IMPLICATIONS OF EVOLUTION, Pergamon Press, p. 150

16 Matthews L. Harrison, Introduction to Darwin's THE ORIGIN OF SPECIES, J.M. Dent & Sons, 1971, p.xi

17 Lipson H.S., *A Physicist Looks at Evolution*, PHYSICS BULLETIN, vol.31, 1980, p. 138

television program[18] he pointed out that scientists "jumped on" Darwin's Origin Of Species because the idea of God was too restrictive to their sexual morals. It is noteworthy that he did not primarily give "scientific" reasons, like "overwhelming evidence", or "convincing proof, but a purely religious reason — dissatisfaction with God's requirements for moral standards." Huxley's well known brother, Aldous, in an article "Confessions of a Professed Atheist", said something very similar:- "We objected to the morality because it interfered with our sexual freedom".

The religious connotations of evolution were expressed very clearly by Ken Wilber in "the Ataman Project" when he said:- "If men and women have come up from amoebas, then they are ultimately on their way towards God".

Obviously.

If man is simply the highest point to which evolution has so far progressed there is no reason to believe that the process stops at man, it must go further, advancing towards the Ultimate. The religious ideas of the "New Age" movement are clearly to be seen here, the concept of the "new man", the next stage in evolution — reaching forward to "the Christ that is within us".

This is actually a very old idea. As Wilber pointed out in "Up From Eden":- "Belief in man's ascension to Godhead is the heart of what has been known as the 'perennial philosophy', the esoteric core of Hinduism, Buddhism, Taoism, Sufism …".

And yet there is the general impression that evolution does, in fact, have something to do with science. Many vigorously claim that it does have a sound scientific basis. To be able to consider anything from a scientific standpoint a definition is essential. In "Evolution and Genetics" the tremendously influential Julian Huxley defined evolution like this :- "Evolution in the extended sense can be defined as a directional and essentially irreversible process occurring in time, which in its course gives rise to an increase of variety and an increasingly high level of organization in its products. Our present knowledge indeed forces us to the view that the whole of reality is evolution — a single process of self- transformation".

Recently evolutionists have begun to shy away from such a clear statement, and reduce their definition essentially to weak, lame, emasculated forms which

---

18 Kennedy D.J., EVOLUTION'S BLOOPERS AND BLUNDERS.

tell us nothing. But Huxley's is a definition which fits what evolution is supposed to be, it specifies what evolution is and what it does. The reason why
any real definition like Huxley's is an embarrassment is that it is so obviously
in conflict, not only with the facts of everyday experience (random accidents
always make things worse, never better), but also with the best established
law of science, the famous "Second Law of Thermodynamics", (which is a
scientific formulation of that same observation).

Isaac Asimov had a talent for expressing complex ideas very simply; he put
the second law of thermodynamics in an easily understandable form when he
said[19] :- "As far as we know all changes are in the direction of increasing
entropy, of increasing disorder, of increasing randomness, of running down".
The second law of thermodynamics is also known as "the fundamental law of
science". It is the only law of science which has never seriously been challenged. There have been feeble challenges though. Some for example have
tried to challenge it by bringing in external energy, by pointing out that the
original formulation of the law actually applied only to "closed systems",
systems in which no external energy enters.

Two very well known evolutionists, George Gaylord Simpson and W.S.
Beck[20], noted that external energy is no way out of the difficulty for evolution when they said:- "But the simple expenditure of energy is not sufficient
to develop and maintain order. A bull in a china shop performs work, but he
neither creates nor maintains organization. The work needed is particular work;
it must follow specifications; it requires information on how to proceed".

The point they are making is that meaningful order, information, the kind of
order demanded by evolution, needs the controlling influence of intelligence.
It needs an energy transformation device designed for the purpose. The second law of thermodynamics deals with systems not influenced by external
intelligence — evolution claims to do the same. Evolutionists get over the
second law in the same way they get over the problem of the origin of life —
by abandoning the basic assumptions of evolution.

A slightly different approach which has been suggested is the possibility that
there may be some situation, somewhere in the universe, where the second

---

19 Asimov I., *Can Decreasing Entropy Exist In The Universe?*, SCIENCE DIGEST,
May 1973.

20 Simpson George G., and Beck W.S., LIFE; AN INTRODUCTION TO BIOLOGY, Harcourt,
Brace & World, 1965, p. 466

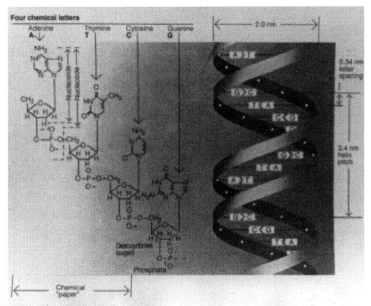

Illustration 28
DNA

The double helix of the DNA molecule is the most efficient information storage and retrieval device known. It is many millions of millions of times more efficient than the best electronic computer chips. (Illustration above by Werner Gitt). No information storage system has ever been observed to form by natural physical or chemical processes - nor has the information stored been observed to generate itself.

In the atomic model (left), each bead represents one atom in the double helix.

law does not always hold. But as H.F. Blum[21] pointed out:- "… the principal reason for accepting the second law of thermodynamics is that it has always worked wherever it has been possible to make the necessary measurements to

21 Blum H.F., TIME'S ARROW AND EVOLUTION, Princeton University Press, 1951, p. 202

test it; we assume therefore that it holds where we are unable to make such measurements". Science is based on measurement. Science says the second law has never been shown to be in error.

There is another reason why the argument that the law might not hold in some forgotten corner of the universe is inadequate. As Huxley pointed out, the evolutionist has to accept that "the whole of reality is evolution". Starting from the total disorder of a primordial explosion, all the order of the entire universe (a closed system) must evolve by itself. The second law must be broken everywhere, not just in some inaccessible corner of the universe.

The second law says that the whole of reality is a self-transformation process downwards. Huxley's definition of evolution says the whole of reality is a self-transformation process upwards. It is exactly 100% opposed to the best established law in the whole of science.

To try to get over the obvious conflict with the second law, more modest definitions were put forward. Professor G.A.Kerkut for example [22] defined the "General Theory of Evolution" as "The theory that all the living forms in the world have arisen from a single source which itself came from an inorganic form."

A problem with this (or any similar definition) was let out of the bag when Kerkut continued ..."the evidence which supports this in not sufficiently strong to allow us to consider it as anything more than a working hypothesis."

It also does not get away from the second law. Although it does not specifically mention increasing order and complexity it requires it since the single source has to generate all known forms of life.

Recently some evolutionists have been turning to the occult ideas of eastern religions, and invoking a universal consciousness pushing the whole of reality towards ever higher levels. One could then suppose that the reason all experiments support the second law is that this consciousness is shy, and stops its upward thrust whenever a scientist takes measurements. One is of course entitled to believe such an idea, but it cannot be considered in any way scientific.

In recognition of the absolute necessity to the theory of evolution of order

22 Kerkut, G.A., IMPLICATIONS OF EVOLUTION, Pergamon, Oxford, UK, p.157,1960.

being spontaneously produced from disorder, some have turned to the mathematical theory of chaos. The name "Chaos" was given by an American, James Yorke, to a mathematical phenomenon actually called "deterministic non-periodicity". "Chaos" is a much easier name to remember, but with typical American aplomb, Yorke chose a word with a completely different meaning. The original name, "deterministic non-periodicity" is an accurate description of the discipline, "chaos" is not. In the original name the "deterministic" indicates that the behaviour is determined by specific equations (which are always non-linear), and "non-periodic", indicates that when certain values are given to the parameters (usually values which take the equations far from equilibrium), the equations do not lead to the sort of simple, repeating (periodic) solutions that scientists like to find.

That hardly seems relevant or supportive to the idea of evolution. As Simpson and Beck pointed out, information is required. Some chaoticians seem to have lent support to evolution by using a definition of "information" given by Claud Shannon[23], another American with little regard for the accepted meaning of words. Shannon's usage has been called a "specialized value-free term without the usual connotations" and "just a fancy word for unpredictability"[24]. Chaos has never shown the possibility of information with the normal meaning of the word being produced by random processes. Information requires the ordering of specified tokens to contain a meaning (for example the dots and dashes in a Morse-code message). Professor Marcel Schutzenberger, Professor of Mathematics at the University of Paris, and former Professor of Mathematical Biology at Harvard University, said of this idea[25] :- "All those who knew Von Forster, the first to have developed this idea, know that it was a joke which some have taken seriously. In fact the orderings which appear are very simple orderings without any relevance to the structures observed in living organisms". If any doubt remains about the theory of chaos giving credibility to evolution, a statement by John Hubbard, one of the leaders in the field of chaos, should dispel the last suspicion. He said:-[26] "There is no randomness in anything that I do. Neither do I think that the possibility of randomness has any direct relevance to biology. In biology

23   Shannon C.E. & Weaver W., *The Mathematical Theory of Communication*, Urbana, University of Illinois, 1963.

24   Gleick J., CHAOS, Heinemann, London, 1988, pp. 255, 261.

25   Schutzenberger, M., *Evolution Condemns Darwin*, FIGARO, 26th October, 1991, p. 84.

26   Quoted in Gleick J., CHAOS p. 239.

randomness is death, chaos is death".

Although the theory of "chaos" has thrown light on such things as dripping taps, crystals and snowflakes, it has not overthrown the second law of thermodynamics — it remains the fundamental law of science — and it remains strictly opposed to evolution.

If evolution is absolutely opposed to the fundamental law of science one might ask how it could ever have been accepted as being in any way "scientific". Evolution entered the realm of speculative "science" through the work of Charles Darwin. Darwin travelled in a ship called the Beagle to South America and the Galapagos Islands, he noticed that in various kinds of creatures there was a range of size, shape and colour. He studied, for example, finches and lizards, and speculated that the variously shaped individuals had all developed from one ancestral type. He was very probably correct, but the observations do not exist to confirm that speculation. A similar range of variation exists in almost all kinds of creature, and since, in some cases, records have been kept, we can examine the situation using a well documented kind. A particularly well documented one is the dog kind.

There are well over a hundred recognized breeds of dog. They range from huge, dangerous hunks of muscle and teeth like the black and tan Rottweiler, to fluffy bundles of fur, like the little white Pomeranian which is happy to

Illustration 29

A great range of size, shape and colour can be observed in most kinds of creature but there are always limits beyond which variation is never observed to go.

curl up on Granny's lap. Despite the great range of variation, all of the various breeds can be traced back to one original wild type called "Tomarctus". The huge range of different breeds of dogs has arisen in a short period of time simply by selection. The genetic potential for all was there in the original wild type, and a competent dog breeder could breed back to Tomarctus simply by crossing various different present-day breeds.

It has been found possible to breed small dogs and big dogs, dogs with long hair or short hair, big ears or small ears, but there are always limits beyond which it is impossible to go. There is a limit to how big a dog can be bred, eventually the breeder finds that the offspring "throw back" to a smaller size. It is impossible to breed a dog as big as an elephant. Similarly there is a limit to how small a dog can be bred, there comes a point where there is a throw back to a larger size. It is impossible to breed a dog as small as a grasshopper. And it has never been found possible to breed a dog with horns, or scales, or feathers, or wings. The only thing it has ever been found possible to breed from a dog is another dog.

Illustration 30

A great variety of pigeons have been bred from wild types in a very short time, illustrating the tremendous potential for variation within a kind. No new organs or structures developed — only variation in existing structures has ever been observed.

Despite the huge range of variation seen in the dog kind, there are other kinds which display an even greater range. Among the birds, for example, it has been noted that from one kind of pigeon it has been possible to breed offspring so different in appearance, temperament and habits that they would have been classed not only as different species, but different genera, if it were not known that they all came from the same original ancestors. This highlights the subjective and unsatisfactory nature of the classification system as well as the amazing capacity for variation within the gene pool of a single kind. Among plants the range of variation is even greater than in animals.

The potential for variation is part of the genetic make-up of every kind of creature.

Darwin speculated that eventually variation would be able to lead to a new kind, to evolution. Although experiment and observation have not supported this speculation, the use of the term "micro-evolution", instead of "variation within a kind", has lent linguistic support to the idea. The variation of colours in peppered moths, for example, is used as an example of "micro-evolution". The use of this term rather suggests that only a slightly bigger step of the same sort is required to produce real evolution or "macro-evolution" as it is now called. But real evolution actually requires something completely different, it requires that an offspring is produced which has some beneficial organ or structure new to the biological world. That has never, ever, been observed to happen. The mechanism which was proposed by which it might, possibly, happen is "mutation".

For many years after the idea of mutation was put forward as the mechanism of evolution scientists could only speculate as to what mutations actually involved. All observed mutations were harmful. They were observed to come in three kinds. The first observed effect of a real mutation is an existing organ or structure in excess or deficit — too many or too few of them. Mutations induced following the Chernobyl disaster have afforded many striking instances; for example, children with no arms or legs. The second observed effect of a real mutation is an existing organ or structure being damaged (sometimes growing in the wrong place). Examples of damaged hands, feet, arms or legs are typical. The third, and final observed result of mutation is the occurrence of "intersexes", creatures which are not normally hermaphrodites, having half of the characteristics of the male, half of the female. These are always naturally sterile. [27]

---

27 Some mutations cause no observable effects. Almost all of these mutations are lethal and do not produce a live offspring to be observed.

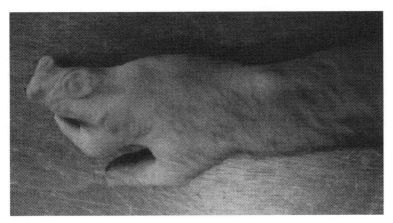

Illustration 32
Observed mutations cause damage to existing organs or structures.

Although observations have shown that mutations never produce anything new, just a damaged version of the original, not knowing what the mechanism of mutation actually was, it was possible to speculate that some mutations might be good, even though no good mutation had ever been observed. But about forty years ago it was discovered that there is a fantastically complex structure to a material called "Deoxyribonucleic acid" which is found in every living cell. That tongue-twister, is, for obvious reasons, usually abbreviated to "DNA". Detailed examination of DNA suggests that it has the form of a "double helix" — two arms of helical shape connected by chemicals called "nucleotides". There are four different kinds of nucleotide, their names are Thiamine, Guanine, Cytosine and Adenine. The sequence of these chemicals on the DNA holds information in exactly the same way that the sequence of "dots" and "dashes" of a message in Morse code does. The well-known expert on information theory, Professor Werner Gitt, Director of Data Processing at the German Institute of Physics and Technology, said of the information storage capability of DNA [28] :- "As a carrier of information the DNA molecule is 45 million million times more efficient than man's 'hi-tech' silicon devices".

The coded information constitutes a program which is believed to direct many, possibly even all, of the workings of the organism. It is considered to be exactly like a computer program of fantastic complexity. The simplest known

---

28 Gitt W., *Information, the Third Fundamental Quantity*, SIEMENS REVIEW, 6/89.

living organism has a program far more complex than any program ever written for an electronic computer. The information in the DNA of an amoeba would fill several hundred thick books. Mutation is accidental change to this program. It has been found that these changes, random mutations, are usually caused by radiation damage or by chemical interference. This knowledge has enabled mathematicians and computer scientists to look into the possibility of random mutations leading to evolutionary progress; the possibility that even though no such progress has ever been observed to happen in reality, it might at least be feasible that it could happen in theory.

In other words, it has become possible to consider the idea from a scientific standpoint, rather than from the point of view of pure speculation.

One of the first scientists to do such an analysis was Professor Marcel Schutzenberger. He was one of the experts invited to address the famous symposium at the Wistar Institute. He said[29] :- "If we try to simulate such a situation by making changes randomly at the typographic level (by letters or by blocks, the size of the unit does not really matter), on computer programs we find that we have no chance (i.e. less than 1 chance in ten to the power one thousand) even to see what the modified program would compute". What he is saying is that it does not matter how big a block of program is randomly altered, there is no chance of evolutionary improvement. And he places a firmer restriction on "no chance" than Borel did, Borel said one chance in 10^{50} is no chance, Schutzenberger would accept one chance in $10^{1\,000}$, and there is still "no chance" that this could possibly happen.[30]

So on theoretical grounds evolution seems to have little credibility. To be of any value at all a scientific theory must make predictions. The theory of evolution has made predictions. Charles Darwin made a prediction in his "Origin of Species'. He said:- "The number of intermediate and transitional links between all living and extinct species must have been inconceivably great. But assuredly, if this theory be true, such have lived upon the earth". Here we see a definite prediction of the theory: intermediate forms. Huxley predicted that those links would certainly be found in the Geological Record.

---

29   Schutzenberger M., MATHEMATICAL CHALLENGES … , pp. 74, 75

30   A single kind of mutation has been observed to give "improvement". That is the case where a mutation reverses a mutation which had damaged a gene. The gene ends up as it was in the beginning before any mutation occurred. There is growing evidence that such correctional changes do not occur by chance but involve an intricate repair mechanism.

A few years ago Professor Stephen Jay Gould, and Dr. Niles Eldredge did a tour in which they put forward their new idea in evolution, "punctuated equilibrium". At one of their meetings in London it was exactly the lack of these links which made the biggest impression on the science correspondent of the "Guardian". He wrote[31] :- "If life had evolved into its wondrous profusion of creatures little by little, Dr. Eldredge argues, then one would expect to find fossils of transitional creatures which were a bit like what went before them and a bit like what came after. But no one has yet found any evidence of such transitional creatures. This oddity has been attributed to gaps in the fossil record which gradualists expected to fill when rock strata of the proper age had been found. In the last decade, however, geologists have found rock layers of all divisions of the last 500 million years and no transitional forms were contained in them".

We seem to have a distinct contradiction of Darwin and Huxley's prediction.

Colin Patterson, a scientist we came across earlier, has also run into this problem. He wrote a book entitled "Evolution" which excited some queries from Luther Sunderland. Answering these he said:- "I fully agree with your comments on the lack of direct illustration of evolutionary transformation in my book. If I knew of any, fossil or living, I would certainly have included them. Yet Gould and the American Museum people are hard to contradict when they say there are no transitional fossils. I will lay it on the line — there is not one such fossil for which one could make a watertight argument". This is quite an admission for a man in charge of one of the finest fossil collections in the world — several million of the very best. It illustrates the difference between a top scientist of Patterson's class, and the second rate scientist that one usually meets. A first class scientist is only content with watertight arguments, second class scientists are often content to put forward arguments which are absolutely "full of holes".

The sort of argument usually used by palaeontologists can be illustrated by considering what would have happened if dogs were now extinct, but fossils of the various breeds of dog had been preserved. The various different shapes and sizes would have been arranged in a sequence from smallest to largest (palaeontologists almost invariably assume that the big evolved from the small). Each breed would have been classed as a different species. With little doubt the Maltese Poodle would not only have been considered a different species to the Great Dane, it would have been classed as a different genus,

---

31 *Missing Believed Non-existent*, The Guardian Weekly, 26 Nov. 1978.

Illustration 33
If lap dogs and hunting dogs had been found only in the fossil record they would
have been classified as different species. Formerly it would almost certainly have
been assumed that the bigger evolved from the smaller. Today it would be more
likely to be assumed that they both evolved from some unknown common ancestor.

one of the Great Dane's "primitive" ancestors. But we actually know that
both the Maltese Poodle and the Great Dane were bred from the intermediate
sized Tomarctus, that it happened in a short space of time, and that it did not
involve evolution at all, but simply illustrates the great capacity within any
"kind" for wide variation. A scientist of Patterson's class is not prepared to
accept weak arguments of this sort, the sort that palaeontologists usually put
forward for evidence of evolutionary transition in the fossil record.

Patterson mentioned "Gould and the American Museum people". Stephen
Jay Gould has been called the "Prince of Evolution". Concerning this problem Gould said[32] :- "The extreme rarity of transitional forms in the fossil record
persists as the trade secret of palaeontology. ... We fancy ourselves as the
only true students of life's history, yet to preserve our favoured account of
evolution by natural selection we view our data as so bad that we never see
the very process we profess to study". Not many scientists appear to be as

32 Gould S.J., *Evolution's erratic pace*, NATURAL HISTORY, vol. 86(5), May 1977.

honest as this, and Gould later seemed to regret that he had let the cat out of the bag, but the truth seems to be that no one has ever seen the evolution that evolutionists profess to study. This lack of intermediate and transitional forms has been such an embarrassment to evolutionists that they have had to conceal the problem with the cunning use of words. Unusual definitions taken from the fields of cladistics and phenetics are used without pointing out the difference from their normal definitions, as used by Darwin and Huxley. It is then possible for evolutionists to say that there are many intermediate and transitional forms, but they do not mean what Darwin meant.

Another interesting prediction of evolution was made by Emil Zukerkandle soon after the structure of DNA had been observed. He predicted that the genes and gene products of "closely related" species would be more similar than those of more "distantly related" species. Colin Patterson addressed this prediction by comparing the proteins of various creatures. He said "The theory makes a prediction, we've tested it, and the prediction is falsified precisely". The genes and gene products of "closely related" species are not usually more similar than those of "distantly related" species. Patterson gave examples where exactly the opposite is true.[33]

Many biologists have accepted that mutations do not provide a mechanism for evolution, as Professor Pierre-Paul Grasse, past president of the French Academy of Sciences, admitted[34] :- "No matter how numerous they may be, mutations do not produce any kind of evolution".

Linguistic revisionism has retained some plausibility for the mutation idea. There are processes called "inversion" and "recombination" which probably occur in every reproduction. Distinct sections of code, called "genes", occasionally swap their positions on the chromosome. There is a well defined probability (generally believed to be one chance in a million) that this may happen for any particular gene. Rearrangement of genes seems to be an important mechanism for giving variation within a kind; it affects such characteristics as colour of eyes, length of hair, etc. It probably explains why each individual is slightly different to every other. Rearrangement of genes is sometimes deceptively referred to as "mutation", with the inference that it explains evolution. Actually this is "permutation" involving only pre-existing

---

33 Less honest evolutionists usually seek out cases which do fit the theory without mentioning the fact that other cases do not.

34 Grasse Pierre-Paul, EVOLUTION OF LIVING ORGANISMS, Academic Press, New York, 1977, p. 88.

units of genetic material, and is irrelevant to evolution.

Evolution requires genetic material to be accidentally created. Inversion and recombination do not explain the formation of new genetic code, and they have never been observed to lead to any evolutionary progress.

Interesting observations have been made which suggest that bacteria and viruses may be able to transfer genetic material from one creature to another. Immunity of bacteria to antibiotics occurs frequently by genetic information being transferred from one bacterium to another by a virus. It has even been suggested that the prime function of viruses may be to allow bacteria (which are essential for the maintenance of the environment as a whole) to survive in different conditions by such transfer of information..

At first sight such transfer of genetic material might seem to hold out great promise for the idea of evolution. Perhaps, for example, a creature with no eyes might receive genetic code needed for the production of an eye via an infecting bacterium. But this would require already existing genetic material for an eye in the donor. It does not explain how the donor came to have an eye in the first place. And in fact, in higher organisms, apart from the possible effect of gaining the ability to produce one of the donor's proteins, it appears that if genetic material is transferred in this way it usually seems to remain dormant. On the rare occasions when foreign DNA does get activated (apart from the cases where it simply allows the production of one of the donor's proteins) it leads to cancer, leukaemia, or some other disaster, but not to evolutionary progress.

Even more interesting is the observation that there are higher control mechanisms than that so far recognized in DNA. Although no mechanism has been fully identified (illustrating how little science really knows at present), it seems there is the capability of actually modifying the DNA in a purposeful way. This seems to be particularly valuable for the immune system. When a new antibody or antitoxin is required it appears that a higher control mechanism can cause duplication of a gene with a code somewhat similar to that which is required. An enzyme then modifies the code to specify the required new antibody. Until a higher control mechanism has been fully identified and examined it will be impossible to gain an idea of the probability of it having arisen by chance. But it seems safe to guess that it will be even less likely that it could have been produced by statistical processes than the known codes of the DNA. An interesting finding concerning the immune system is that very restricted areas of genetic code can be stimulated to mutate very quickly and thus perform a random search for a key to match that of a disease-causing invader. This has to be under strict control, because if such mutation occurred anywhere else in the DNA it would rapidly lead to error catastrophe and death. The more scientists find out about living organisms the more amazing and complex they are seen to be and the more vividly they appear to show evidence of skilful design.

Between genes coding for proteins there are sections of code whose function is not yet known. Such code was initially given the name "junk code", implying that it was useless. Some suggested that it was left over from previous evolution. This is reminiscent of the "Vestigial organ" story. More than a hundred organs in the human body alone were once labelled vestigial and said to have no use. One by one their functions have been discovered. There is evidence already that some of the "junk code" has vital functions such as checking the accuracy of the copying of genetic information.

In spite of all the uncertainties and the exciting possibilities hinted at by such recent findings, observations consistently show no Darwinian evolution. One can observe variation within a kind certainly, but never outside the kind. And the more science finds out, the more clear it becomes that naturalistic chance processes are totally inadequate to explain not only the existence of life in any form, but also any progress from one form to another.

The famous scientist Professor Sir Fred Hoyle, after thorough examination of the possibility of random changes leading to evolutionary advance, expressed his conclusions in a form more forceful and easily understood than Professor Schutzenberger's; he said[35] :- "The chance that higher life forms might have emerged in this way is comparable with the chance that a tornado sweeping through a junk-yard might assemble a Boeing 747 from the materials therein". And that, of course, is simply another way of saying "absolutely no chance at all".

Another well respected scientist, Lee Spetner, an information science expert and bio-physicist who spent years working on the feasibility of evolution has come to the conclusion that however the living things around us came to be here it was certainly NOT BY CHANCE.[36]

---

35 Hoyle Sir Fred, as quoted in *Hoyle on Evolution*, NATURE, vol.294, 12 Nov. 1981 p. 105

36   Lee Spetner; NOT BY CHANCE; Judaica Press; NY; ISBN 1-880582-24-4); 1996.

If evolution has no defensible mechanism and less than no chance at all of being true, what then can be said of all the evidence that supposedly proves the theory? It seems that much is speculation based on the preconceived ideas of scientists who believe the theory so firmly that they see what they *want* to see. Just as Professor Osborne deceived himself in seeing the evolution of man in a wild pig's tooth, others have deceived themselves also. The evidence for evolution seems to be largely speculation and story-telling. As Dr. Colin Patterson said in a television interview[37] :- "… the narratives about change over time, how the dinosaurs became extinct, how the mammals evolved, where man came from. These seem to me to be little more than story-telling".

Professor Louis Bournoure, former director of research at the French National Centre of Scientific Research, agreed when he said[38] :- "Evolution is a fairy tale for grown-ups. This theory has helped nothing in the progress of science. It is useless". The well-known Scandinavian scientist Soren Lovtrup, in his book "Darwinism, the Refutation of a Myth" went further than this and said:- "I believe that one day the Darwinian myth will be ranked the greatest deceit in the history of science". Malcolm Muggeridge, in one of the Pascal Lectures at the university of Waterloo, Ontario, Canada said:- "I myself am convinced that the theory of evolution, especially the extent to which it's been applied, will be one of the great jokes in the history books of the future. Posterity will marvel that so very flimsy and dubious an hypothesis could be accepted with the incredible credulity that it has".

Then how can it be that there are many who still seem to believe in the theory?

Many are simply second rate scientists who either do not keep up with the current findings, or fail to consider seriously the meaning of observations. But there is a far more important reason. Professor Giuseppe Sermonti, professor of genetics at Perugia University, in an interview with Jean Staune said[39] :- "If I am interested in combating Darwinism it is not that it is a false theory — there are many false theories throughout the world — it is because it is dishonest. What shocked me also is that the supporters of Darwinism do not believe it themselves". Jean Staune responded:- "But Ernst Mayr believes it!" (Mayr is, of course, an extremely famous proponent of evolution). Sermonti answered:- "But he is a Bishop, a High Priest of the theory, he has to give the

---

37 Patterson Colin, B.B.C. Television interview 4 March 1982.

38 Bounoure L., as quoted in THE ADVOCATE, Thursday 8 March 1984, p. 17.

39 *Evolution Condemns Darwin*, FIGARO, 26 Oct.1991.

impression that he believes it. I don't think that when he returns to his room, alone with himself, he really believes that little accidental mutations and natural selection could suffice to produce a dinosaur from an amoeba. It is not possible that he believes that".

Sermonti's use of "Bishop" and "High Priest of the theory" are revealing. Evolution is, as noted earlier, essentially a religious idea. The fact that science has demonstrated the theory to be untenable apparently makes little difference to a believer.

Michael Denton, in "Evolution: A Theory In Crisis", concluded by saying[40] :- "The truth is that despite the prestige of evolutionary theory, and the tremendous intellectual effort directed towards reducing living systems to the confines of Darwinian thought ... the origin of new beings on earth is still largely as enigmatic as when Darwin set sail on the Beagle".

But it is possible to go further than that. We can be confident that there is less than no chance that the beings on the earth are the result of evolution. We can see why the well-known physicist Professor H.S. Lipson said[41] :- "I think, however, that we must go further than this and admit that the only acceptable explanation is creation. I know that this is anathema to physicists, as indeed it is to me, but we must not reject a theory that we do not like if the experimental evidence supports it."

Creation is anathema to many physicists ... and biologists, and palaeontologists, and indeed to all humanists. Wernher von Braun, the famous scientist who led the American space program, put his finger on the heart of the matter when he pointed out that creation is impossible without a creator. Humanists do not like the idea of a creator — as Huxley pointed out, it implies, among other things, standards for sexual morals.

But whether God's standards of moral behaviour are considered to be onerous or not, there is a question which needs to be taken seriously. With Darwin's theory "nonsense of a high order", "a fairy tale for grown ups", "the greatest deceit in the history of science" and "one of the great jokes in the history books of the future", if there is no creator, then how on earth did we get here?

---

40 Denton Michael, EVOLUTION: A THEORY IN CRISIS, Adler and Adler, 1986, pp. 358–359.

41 Lipson H.S., *A Physicist Looks at Evolution*, PHYSICS BULLETIN, Vol.31, 1980, p. 138.

Chapter 5

When Did It All Begin?

When it comes to the question of when the universe came into being, practically all educated people presume that the astronomers must have cast-iron proof for the thousands of millions of years which they bandy about as established fact. Closer examination suggests, though, that there is room for doubt. Based on the Big Bang Hypothesis the most popular estimates for the age of the Universe range from ten to twenty thousand million years. We have already seen in Chapter 2 that there is serious doubt about the reliability of the Big Bang, so we might have reservations about accepting the estimates of age based on it. In fact we do not need to look very far before we find great difficulties for such an age.

Spiral galaxies are believed to be huge islands of stars swirling round in space. The appearance seems to suggest two or more arms of gas, dust and stars gradually being wound around a centre. At the speed the stars in the galaxies are believed to be moving, those near the centre should have orbited about a hundred times more often than those near the edge. The galaxies should have wound themselves up to become flat uniform disks of gas, dust and stars.

But they are not, the spiral structure is clear, and there are usually only one, one and a half, perhaps two turns in the spiral. As usual though, this does not necessarily mean that the great age has to be abandoned. A valiant ad hoc attempt has been made by proposing that spiral galaxies are indeed effectively flat disks:- the spiral appearance is just a passing phase caused by some kind of pressure wave of spiral form sweeping through the disk, somehow causing stars to form and giving the temporary appearance of spiral arms. Unfortunately for that idea though, it has been shown that such a pressure wave could never form. Even if a pressure wave could somehow be produced it would fade away quite quickly. Stretching one's imagination, such an idea might, perhaps, account for a galaxy or two. But there are millions.

Another ad hoc has stars exploding in sequence outwards from the centre and inducing new stars to form due to the shock. The details are fuzzy, and unconfirmed by any kind of experimental evidence, but it is a fairly logical extension of the Big Bang theory in that it assumes that explosions lead to constructive processes. Some calculations suggest that ongoing star formation can stabilise spiral structure. But unless the temperature is below 5 degrees absolute clouds of gas and dust have more energy tending to drive them apart than gravitational energy tending to draw them together. Temperatures

Illustration 34
Spiral Galaxy

There are millions of spiral galaxies like this. They are believed to consist of millions of stars swirling around a centre. The spiral rarely shows more than two turns from the centre to the edge. This suggests that they cannot be very old.

of gas and dust in the spiral galaxies are far higher, so to propose star formation there we need some unobserved and unlikely mechanism to generate them. But without bringing in such ad hocs, spiral galaxies suggest a maximum age at least a hundred times younger than that given by the Big Bang even if the arms were perfectly straight, without any spiral structure, when they were created.

Observations have convinced the astronomers that galaxies do not occur singly, but only in groups or "clusters". These clusters often contain many galaxies, sometimes hundreds.

All these galaxies seem to be swirling around at enormous speed, and moving in such a way that within quite a short time they should have dispersed, or separated from each other. Within a short time there should have been no clusters of galaxies left, just single galaxies randomly wandering through space. Then how is it possible to continue believing the clusters are thousands of millions of years old? The most popular solution is to assume that there must be vast amounts of mass in the clusters which cannot be detected, and the gravity of that invisible material holds everything together. Since there is no evidence for this mass it is usually called the "missing mass". It is not just a little of the mass which is missing … in the famous Virgo cluster, for example, more than 90% of the mass needed to hold it together is missing. Some observations can only be explained by assuming at least 99% of the required mass is missing! Many suggestions have been put forward as to what form the missing mass might take, but one by one they have been shown to be untenable. A serious consequence of the idea of missing mass is that according to the Big Bang theory, its presence reduces the age of the universe — the more missing mass, the younger the universe has to be — another major problem for the standard ideas of astronomy.

Illustration 35
Globular Cluster
Globular clusters are believed to be the oldest astronomical objects. A number of observations suggest that they cannot be very old.

Without bringing in ad hocs like missing mass it seems that the maximum possible age for clusters of galaxies is several thousand times less than the Big Bang's age.

Globular Clusters are believed to be among the oldest astronomical objects. They are thought to be huge collections of stars (up to a million of them) all packed into a sphere. There appear to be over a hundred of these clusters which are believed to be close to the centre of the Milky Way Galaxy. They also present huge problems for the vast ages of the Big Bang Universe. For a start there are some which appear to be hurtling away from the galaxy at such a rate that they ought to have disappeared long ago — or if they are there because they are passing through, and had just grazed the Milky Way, they should have been distorted by the gravitational pull of the galaxy's dense nucleus. But they are spherical, not distorted. Many are thought to be orbiting the dense nucleus of the galaxy at such speeds that they should pass through the plane of the galaxy's disk about every ten million years. The disk of the galaxy is believed to be full of gas, dust and stars. The gravitational pull of the galaxy and the repeated collisions with the disk should have distorted the clusters within a comparatively short time. But they are all still beautifully spherical. Each star in the cluster is believed to be a sun like ours, giving off a "solar wind" of gas and dust. The accumulated gas from the solar wind of hundreds of thousands of stars should be easily detectable but no gas or dust has been found in the globular clusters. Interesting ad hocs have been devised to explain this away. The most intriguing considers that each time a globular cluster passes through the dust clouds of the galaxy's disk its gas and dust are swept out and the cluster emerges sparkling clean, in much the same way that one's best suit might be cleaned very effectively by dragging it through an ash heap! Unfortunately for that idea though, some of the clusters are in such a position that if they have ever passed through the galaxy's disk it must have been so long ago that, even if they had been "dust cleaned", they would be full of gas again by now. On several counts it seems that these "old" astronomical objects are actually not very old at all. Without bringing in ad hocs it looks as if the maximum age possible for globular clusters is several thousand times less than the age assigned by currently popular theories.

Within the galaxy is a different kind of star cluster called "Galactic Clusters" or "Open Clusters". Practically all of them seem to be flying apart rapidly. This is another aspect of the missing mass problem; there appears to be not enough mass to hold the clusters together. There does, however, seem to be an exception — the Pleiades — which the astronomers refer to as a "bound" cluster. It appears that there is enough mass within the Pleiades to bind it together and prevent it from disrupting. An intriguing point that can be noted here is that in the Bible, when God was speaking to Job out of the whirlwind (Job 38 v.31) He asked:- "Canst thou bind the sweet influences of Pleiades, or loose the bands of Orion". That question took on a new aspect for astronomers just a few years ago when they calculated that the Pleiades cluster is, as they put it, "bound". And another interesting point about that same passage is that it would certainly appear that Orion's bands have been loosed, the various groups of stars in the constellation are disrupting rapidly.

Illustration 36
Pleiades
The Pleiades, a beautiful cluster popularly known as the "Seven Sisters", believed to be the only galactic cluster which is not flying apart.

One of Orion's clusters is a famous group called the "Trapezium". The Trapezium is flying apart so quickly that ten thousand years ago its stars would all have been touching. Taking the evidence at face value, without bringing in ad hocs again, it looks as if this cluster suggests an age of only thousands of years rather than millions.

Comets are fairly small bodies, ten kilometres or so in diameter. It is quite

Illustration 37
Part of the constellation of Orion
The horse head nebula can be seen near the centre. The trapezium is lower down,
but hidden by the glow. All the clusters of stars are flying apart rapidly. At the rate the
trapezium is disrupting all its stars would have been touching 10 000 years ago.

likely that they are made up of rocks and dust held together by ice. A famous
American astronomer, Fred Whipple, gave them the name "dirty snowballs".
They seem to come in two kinds, short period and long period. The short
period comets orbit the sun taking from a few years to a few hundred years
for each circuit. The long period comets have very distorted or "eccentric"
orbits which carry them many millions of kilometres away from the sun so
that they should return only after a very long period of time. Comets are too
small to be seen normally, but when they come close to the sun they are
heated and some of the ice melts. Evaporation takes place, dust is set free,
and the solar wind carries material away into space. It is the material evapo-
rated from a comet and blown away by the solar wind which makes a comet
visible. A typical comet at full visibility has a tail about a million kilometres
wide and many millions of kilometres long. The tail is made of material being
blown away into space and lost to the comet for ever. A comet like Halley's
loses about ten tons of material every second throughout the period when it is
visible. Such a small body cannot lose material at such a rate for millions of

years. Analysis shows that short period comets cannot last longer than a few thousand years before they disintegrate completely. But there are still some short period comets left. This would seem to suggest that if, as is generally believed, the comets were formed at the same time as the rest of the Solar System, then the system itself can only be a few thousand years old. To get over this difficulty for the standard theories of age, long period comets are usually brought into the story. A Dutch astronomer, Jan Oort, came up with an ingenious idea. Perhaps there is a huge cloud of comets (many thousands of millions of them) circling the solar system (but, unfortunately, so far away that they cannot be seen or detected in any way). Perhaps also a passing star (which, sadly, cannot be seen or detected either, though it has been given the name "Nemesis") occasionally disturbs the comet cloud and sends a large number of them racing in towards the sun. Perhaps, also, Jupiter is just in the right place to catch some of these comets in its gravitational field and change their orbits in such a way that they become short period comets. Now we would have an explanation for the fact that the existing comets, which cannot be more than a very few thousand years old, can still be here, but the solar system can be much older. Unfortunately for that attractive ad hoc, calculations have shown that the orbits of the existing comets could never have resulted from such a scenario.[1] Surprisingly though, many astronomers still appear to believe in Oort's Cloud. For a while another source of comets was proposed "The Kuyper Belt" named after another Dutch astronomer, but when it became clear it was not a plausible candidate the Oort cloud came back into fashion. No one seems to have come up with a more plausible way of maintaining credibility for the great age for the solar system.

Besides large bodies like comets, the solar system contains a great deal of dust. Analysis shows that dust in the solar system should spiral in toward the sun and be burned up. There is a phenomenon called "Zodiacal Light", which can be seen as a faint glow near the horizon after sunset and before sunrise. It is believed that this is due to dust being swept into the sun. About eight tons of dust are swept into the sun every second. Analysis shows that it would take only a few thousand years for the sun to sweep the solar system clean. Unless there is a source bringing in new dust this suggests that the solar system cannot be more than a few thousand years old. Fred Whipple pointed[2] out

---

1   Littleton R.A., *The Non-existence of the Oort Cometary Shell*, ASTROPHYSICS AND SPACE SCIENCE; Vol.31 1974, pp. 44–47.

2   Whipple Fred L., *On Maintaining the Meteoric Complex*; THE ZODIACAL LIGHT AND THE INTERPLANETARY MEDIUM; NASA SP-150, 1967.

that there is no evidence that any dust is coming from outside the solar system. The amount of dust that could be produced inside the solar system by comets is far too small to explain the zodiacal light. There seems to be no convincing alternative to the deduction that the solar system cannot be more than a few thousand year old.

The space probes sent to the planets have been a source of surprise to scientists. They showed major flaws in their theories. Jupiter had been believed to be very cold. It is not, it is hot. The heat apparently cannot come from any known source, such as radioactivity or gravitational contraction. It looks as if the only explanation is that Jupiter was created recently and has not had time to cool down yet. Io, one of Jupiter's moons, has enormous volcanoes which eject vast quantities of material with such force that much material is thrown out of its gravitational field into space and lost to Io for ever. Io is quite a small body, only about as big as our moon. If this volcanic action had been going on for very long Io must have been very large in the past, and the space around its orbit should be littered with vast quantities of ejected material.

Saturn is also far hotter than the astronomers had predicted. The details of its ring system are also very far from their predictions. The rings consist of millions of ice-covered particles, each in its own orbit around Saturn. Some of the particles are as small as grains of sand, others are as large as a city block; on average they are about as big as a car. Before Voyager reached Saturn, Brad Schaeffer of the team at NASA predicted that the rings would give no surprises. He said this because extensive analysis had been done which showed that unless the rings were in a very specific configuration it would be impossible for them to be stable, they would soon collapse. Voyager showed that the rings are completely different to their expectations. They are not in a stable arrangement. It is hard to see how they can be old.

There is a gap in the rings of Saturn called "Cassini's Division", named after the astronomer who discovered it. This division separates the bright inner ring, known as the "B" ring from the bright outer ring known as the "A" ring. Before Voyager shattered their theories the astronomers had calculated that the division was due to the four closest moons of Jupiter, which were all in "harmonic orbits" with Cassini's division. Each time the moons circle Saturn they should sweep out a little of the material in this division. It had been calculated that the four moons would have swept Cassini's division completely clean within one hundred thousand years. Such was the confidence that Saturn and its rings were far older than a hundred thousand years that Voyager was programmed to skip through Cassini's division and take photographs of the rings on either side. But when Voyager drew close enough to send back detailed pictures of the rings, NASA's team saw to their horror that Cassini's division was far from empty, there was still plenty of material there. The moons did not seem to have had time to sweep the division clean yet. The plans had to be changed, Voyager was re-programmed to pass Saturn inside the rings close to the planet's surface — a very risky procedure. The scien-

Illustration 38
Saturn
Cassini's division can be seen as an apparently empty space between the bright A and B rings. Calculations had shown that it should have been swept clean in less than 100 000 years. Voyager discovered that the division is far from empty.

tists realised there was a good chance of losing their spacecraft, but they knew that losing it was an absolute certainty in Cassini's division. They were lucky: it passed the planet unscathed. Ad hoc theories have been advanced to explain away the obvious inference that the rings cannot be very old.

But before Voyager visited Saturn there was already considerable evidence that the rings are not stable and cannot be very old. The rings are collapsing, drifting down onto the planet's surface.[3] The Russian astronomer Vsekhsviatsky proposed an ad hoc to explain how Saturn and its rings can nevertheless be older than a few thousand years.

---

3 Struve Otto., *Planets With Rings*, SKY AND TELESCOPE; July 1960 pp. 20–23.

He suggested that volcanoes on Saturn must throw up material to form new rings. Analysis shows that even if there were volcanoes which could throw material out so quickly that it could get into orbit, the speed would have to be so high that the material would be burned up by friction in Saturn's dense atmosphere. The observed orbits could not result from such a mechanism anyway. The most reasonable explanation seems to be that the ring system, which was probably created at the same time as the planet, is a short term phenomenon. It cannot last very long.

It cannot have been there very long.

But what of the stars? Can we not get some idea of when it all began by examining them? The Big Bang theory assumes that stars are formed when clouds of gas and dust contract and heat up. Astronomers have shown that unless a cloud of gas and dust has a temperature less than five degrees absolute (minus two hundred and sixty-eight degrees Celsius), the thermal energy tending to make the cloud fly apart is far greater than the gravitational energy

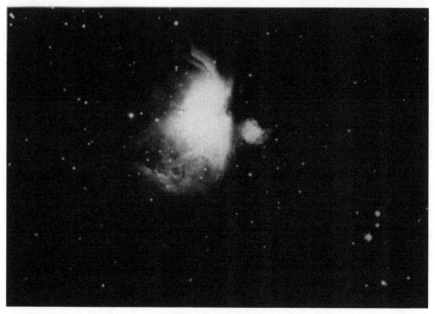

Illustration 39
Great Nebula in Orion
The Great Nebula in Orion is thought to consist of clouds of gas and dust where stars are forming. But the temperature of the gas and dust is far too high to allow contraction. They must, rather, be expanding.

tending to make it contract. The clouds of gas and dust where the astronomers tell us they think stars must be forming are much warmer than this, so star formation would appear to be impossible. Further back in time, astronomers tell us, everything was hotter than it is now … the universe is supposed to be expanding and cooling down. So it was even more impossible for gas and dust to contract and form stars in the past than it is today. Nevertheless we are assured that it must happen. Eventually the temperature in the contracting cloud becomes so high that nuclear reactions begin and a star is born.

The nuclear reactions lead to heavy elements like oxygen, iron and carbon being formed, hence the composition of the star is slowly changed. As the composition changes the star evolves from one kind to another. The colour and temperature gradually change as the millions of years go by. Some swell up to become huge "Red Giants". As the nuclear fuel is used up they contract again and become smaller and hotter. Some eventually explode and become "novas" or "supernovas". The remainder continue to get smaller until they become "White Dwarfs". With all the fuel used up the white dwarf gradually cools and fades from view. Each stage in this evolutionary progression takes vast numbers of years. The whole process takes thousands of millions of years.

Sirius is the brightest star in the sky, and has been observed by astronomers since the dawn of history. All their observations until 150 A.D. are consistent with its being a Red Giant. But all the observations from 1000 A.D. onwards are consistent with its being blue-white[4] as it is today. Sirius has apparently changed from red to white in less than a thousand years. That would tend to throw considerable doubt on the theory of stellar evolution. In 1991 Crosswell made a report in the "New Scientist" about a star called "F G Sagittae"[5]. Observations showed that it changed from a blue star with a temperature of twelve thousand degrees to a yellow star with a temperature of only five thousand degrees in just thirty-six years. Since then it has turned orange, then red, and apparently changed its composition.

A colloquium in 1997 was told "a whole new bunch of spectral lines appeared due to elements such as Sr, Y, Zr, Ba and rare earths." Now the theory of stellar evolution does not normally allow elements like this to suddenly appear (apparently from deep within the interior).

---

4   Maran Stephen, in *It's About Time*; GEOTIMES; Sept. 1978 p. 19.

5   Crosswell K., NEW SCIENTIST; 14th Sept. 1991 pp. 28–41.

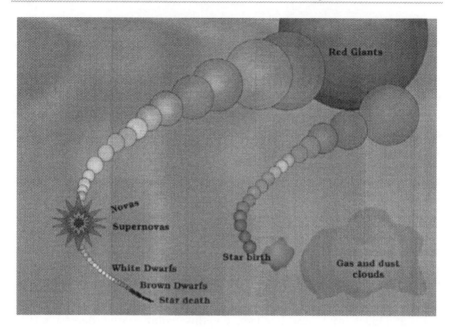

Illustration 40
Stellar Evolution

The story of stellar evolution requires many millions of years.

An article in "Mercury" March/April 1998 noted that F G Sagittae's spectrum changed and suddenly indicated the star was poor in hydrogen and rich in carbon. The same article pointed out that other stars have recently been seen to change spectral type and apparent composition very quickly also.

Of course, ad hoc explanations have been put forward to explain why stellar evolution should proceed so quickly in the case of FG Sagitae. But why should we believe that any star cannot change quickly. After all, there is not one star which has been observed for ten thousand years, never mind ten million. How do we know any of them take a long time to "evolve".

There is another observation which could be related to this problem. The existence of spectral lines indicating Technetium in the atmosphere of stars. Technetium is radioactive, with a short half life; it soon decays away. Stellar evolution theory does not usually allow elements made in the centre of stars to come to the surface, so the atmosphere of the star (which dictates which spectral lines are visible), must consist of elements which were there when the star formed from its gas and dust cloud. If that is so, and there is still Technetium in the atmosphere it cannot have formed very long ago.

The theory of stellar evolution, with its thousands of millions of years, appears to be far from well-supported by observation.

And what about the sun? Until about 1915 almost all scientists believed that the sun (and the stars) produce heat and light by gravitational contraction. Von Helmholtz had shown, and Lord Kelvin had verified, that all the radiation observed could be produced by contraction alone. But there was a problem with this explanation. The theory of evolution had become popular, and all scientists realised that for organic evolution to be possible thousands of millions of years were need. Gravitational contraction could only provide heat and light for a small fraction of that time. Either the sun would have to start off so large that it would have annihilated the earth, or it would have shrunk to a tiny remnant long ago. In 1915 it was proposed that perhaps there might be nuclear reactions in the centre of the sun and stars. Calculations showed that IF there were nuclear reactions inside the sun and stars then they would be able to shine for thousands of millions of years. The next step was the assume that there MUST be nuclear reactions in the sun and stars. Now we are told there ARE nuclear reactions in the sun and stars.

A few years ago it was observed that the sun is pulsating. Calculations done on those pulsations showed that conditions inside the sun cannot be as the theory requires. In particular they throw doubt on whether the temperature in the sun can be hot enough for nuclear reactions to take place. Scientists decided that it would be wise to check their assumption of such reactions. They agreed that if there are nuclear reactions in the sun then those reactions must produce electron neutrinos. A neutrino detector was built, the famous Brookhaven laboratory at the Homestakes gold mine in America. When it was put into commission the scientists found to their horror that it could not detect the neutrinos that were supposed to come from the sun. A few neutrinos were detected, but some had been expected from other sources, so it was doubtful that even those few came from the sun. Doubt was expressed about the ability of the apparatus to detect neutrinos, but in 1987 it detected a sudden burst of them. Astronomers were alerted to look for something unusual, and immediately the famous supernova known as "1987 A" was discovered in the large Magellanic Cloud. The Brookhaven neutrino detector was the first apparatus on earth to detect the supernova. It certainly seems to be able to detect neutrinos, but it cannot detect the neutrinos which are supposed to be coming from the sun. It was then suggested that the sun might produce a different energy neutrino to that which the Brookhaven apparatus could detect. The Gallex detector was built to detect the "right kind". Despite stretching the results there were far too few detected, and those could have come from the other sources anyway. Other detectors have been built, but they have also found far fewer than the required neutrinos. So important is the question that an even more sophisticated detector was built at Sudbury in Canada. In June 2001 the scientists at the Sudbury Neutrino Observatory announced that they had solved the mystery of the missing neutrinos The solution they claimed is that the electron neutrinos produced by the sun change into tau and muon neutrinos on their way from the sun to the detector.. On April 20, 2002 the Sudbury scientists announced new results which, they say, makes it 99.999% certain that this is so. Now that is something that current atomic theory does not allow It will be interesting to see whether the Sudbury explanation or current atomic theory proves more acceptable to the physicists of the world. If it turns out to be the atomic theory which is acknowledged to be faulty, it will be yet another example of well established "truth" showing itself to be unreliable after all. And if atomic theory is in doubt there should be even more doubt about the solar nuclear reactions predicted by that very theory. We might also ask why the Sun's neutrinos change to another kind in their 8 minute flight from the sun, while those from supernovas, vastly further away do not. Perhaps the astronomers will have to have them conveniently changing back to the right kind in time to agree with the Brookhaven observations. Altogether it would seem to have been more reasonable for the Sudbury scientists to say that IF the current theory of energy generation in the sun is correct THEN there is a 99.99% certainty. And that theory will remain impossible to verify until scientists can actually get some apparatus into the sun to check it.

As it happens several scientists have pointed out that measurements of the diameter of the sun suggest that it is shrinking[6]. Perhaps Helmholtz and Kelvin were right in the first place. Or perhaps there is a completely different explanation. A scientist called Bruce has for years suggested that the sun's energy comes from continuous lightning discharges near the surface of the sun. Another scientist called Aspden has suggested that the sun could be a large, stable example of "ball-lightning". Neither theory has ever been shown

6 Lubkin G.B., *Analysis of Historical Data Suggests Sun is Shrinking*; PHYSICS TODAY, Sept. 1979, pp. 17–19. Also Dunham D.W. et al., *Observations of a Probable Change in the Solar Radius Between 1715 and 1979*; SCIENCE, Vol. 210.

to be wrong — but, like the others, they have not been proved correct either.

Altogether it seems that there is no satisfactory model of the sun or the stars, and it is quite probable that the whole theory of stellar evolution is just an interesting speculation. Its vast ages are also speculation.

Reports for the man in the street usually suggest that the thousands of millions of years and nuclear reactions are established fact. The astronomers themselves, however, have known otherwise for many years. In the conference at Louisiana State University mentioned in Chapter 3 [7], scientists looked into some of the many indications that the accepted time scale is unreliable. Among them was Dr. John A. Eddy, one of the world's top experts on the sun. It is worth repeating what he said there:- "I suspect ... that the sun is 4.5 billion years old. However, given some new and unexpected results to the contrary, and some time for frantic readjustment, I suspect that we could live with Bishop Ussher's value for the age of the Earth and Sun. I don't think we have much in the way of observational evidence in astronomy to conflict with that."

Bishop Ussher got his value (about 6 000 years) by counting back the generations in the Bible. If there is not much in the way of observational evidence against this, one might be tempted to ask why one should rather place one's confidence in the suspicions of theorists who have often been proved wrong in the past.

It seems that as far as science is concerned the question of when it all began is very far from settled.

---

[7] Kasman R., *It's About Time*; GEOTIMES, Sept.1978, pp. 18–20.

Chapter 6

Where In The Universe Are We?

Good question! Where, indeed, in the Universe are we?

The currently accepted view among almost all scientists is that we inhabit a second class planet called the Earth, which moves round a second class star called the Sun, which circles round a second class galaxy called the Milky Way, which circles round a second class cluster of galaxies called the Local Cluster which is lost in the vastness of space, like a grain of sand in the Sahara Desert. This is called the "Mediocrity Principle" or the "Copernican Principle". It expresses the way that science now sees our place in the Universe.

But it was not always like that. The ancients had a completely different picture of our position. They considered that the Earth was stationary and everything else in the universe circled round it. That idea came from believing the obvious … believing what their own eyes, their own senses, told them to be true. The earth was obviously not moving, whereas everything else obviously was.

That idea, or some modification of it, hung on in the thoughts of most educated people (including scientists) right until the sixteenth century. One reason was that most of the educated people of the world, and in particular the scientists, were in Europe, which at that time was at least nominally Christian. At least nominally the Bible was taken as the absolute authority. And there seemed to be a great deal of evidence in the Bible to support this Geocentric (earth-centred) picture. So much so that all Bible scholars up to that time were convinced that the Bible taught geocentricity.

The very first verse in the Bible says:- "In the beginning God created the

heaven and the earth". The other bodies in the universe were created later —
on the fourth day. Genesis 1:16:- "And God made two great lights; the greater
light to rule the day, and the lesser light to rule the night: he made the stars
also". So the sun, moon and stars are later additions … and obviously periph-
eral.

The reason for the creation of these heavenly bodies is specifically given:-
Genesis 1:14–15:- "And God said, Let there be lights in the firmament of the
heaven to divide the day from the night; and let them be for signs, and for
seasons, and for days, and years: And let them be for lights in the firmament
of the heaven to give light upon the earth: and it was so." Apparently they
were made solely for the benefit of the earth.

By contrast, we are told that the earth was created specifically for life, as the
rest of Genesis 1 shows, and as stated in Isaiah 45:18:- "For thus saith the
LORD that created the heavens; God himself that formed the earth and made
it; he hath established it, he created it not in vain, he formed it to be inhab-
ited."

Such Scriptures were taken as showing the earth to have a special place and a
special purpose.

Scripture was also taken as giving support to the idea that the earth did not
move whereas everything else did. For example Judges 5 v. 20 talks of the
"stars in their courses", Psalm 19 talks of the sun "running his race" from one
end of the heavens to the other. These and many other such verses seemed to
support the idea that the earth is stationery at the centre, while all the other
heavenly bodies move round it. It is not just in-
dividual verses which give this impression, the
whole tone of the Bible is Geocentric.

Illustration 41
Ptolemy

But there was a problem with the geocentric picture (or "model") of an-
cient times, the model in
which the moon, the sun,
the planets and the stars
moved around the earth

in perfect circles. The model did not fit the observed facts of astronomy. It had to be modified. Ptolemy, a Greek astronomer who worked in Alexandria, found a modification that would make the model fit the observed facts quite well. He considered the heavenly bodies to orbit the epicentre, a point slightly offset from the earth. And instead of having them moving in simple circles, he had them performing what he called "epicycles":- they circled round a point which was itself circling the centre of the universe. Ptolemy refined this

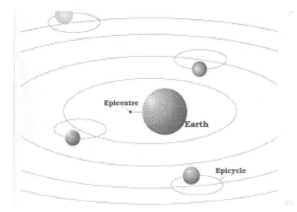

Illustration 42
Ptolemaic System

Ptolemy considered the Earth to be slightly offset from the centre of the universe. Each of the heavenly bodies performs an epicycle around a point moving around the centre in a perfect circle.

model until its predictions were as accurate as the observations of his day.

There did not seem to be too much wrong with this model apart from the fact that it took a good mathematician to do the calculations. It could predict the positions of the sun, moon and planets, and the times of eclipses, to the accuracy of the astronomical observations. There was little really sound scientific reason for abandoning this model until the advent of the telescope allowed more accurate observations to be made.

But long before that happened, the beginning of the sixteenth century saw the Renaissance. This rebirth of interest in the culture of ancient Greece took hold of the philosophers of Europe. The ancient Greeks were essentially humanists. They had a somewhat incongruous pantheon of gods which could be added into any story as and when required, but they could be left out if necessary — it was actually human reason which held the answers to all questions open to philosophical enquiry.

One of the scientists involved in the Renaissance was Nicholas Copernicus. He was particularly interested in Plato and in Pythagoras.

Plato considered that the sun was the embodiment of everything good and noble in the universe.

Pythagoras considered that the sun should be the centre because it is the most magnificent of the gods.

A good, sound scientific reason for making the sun the centre of the universe, and that is exactly what Copernicus did. He proposed a model in which the planets and the stars move round the sun. On this model the earth is simply an ordinary planet. To explain the observations, the earth must rotate about its axis once each day. Astronomy books, and history books also, tend to give the impression that as soon as Copernicus put this idea forward, the problems of astronomy were solved. This is in fact not true. To agree with observations Copernicus had to make the planets follow a more complex system of epicycles than Ptolemy's. As Professor Otto Neugebauer pointed out[1], "the popular belief that Copernicus' heliocentric system constitutes a simplification of the Ptolemaic system is obviously wrong .... the Copernican models themselves require about twice as many circles as the Ptolemaic models".

Not only was it not simpler, it was not more accurate either! Clark noted[2] :-
"The Copernican construction could not predict or describe so accurately as the Ptolemaic system. Scientific observation was definitely more favourable to the old than to the new. But science is not all observation. Copernicus

Illustration 43

Nicholas Copernicus

rejected Ptolemy on aesthetic grounds and not because of any failure to account for the observed facts, yet, when he arrived at his own conclusions, he took the position that at last the real truth had been found".

This is quite a common position in science. When James Hutton and Charles Lyell put for-

---

1 Neugebauer O., as quoted in THE CONFLICT THESIS AND COSMOLOGY, The Open University, 1979, p. 65

2 Clark, Gordon H., THALES TO DEWEY, Trinity Foundation, 1989

ward the uniformitarian explanation of geology (which called for millions of years of Earth history) it did not account for many of the observations as convincingly as the former interpretation (creation and catastrophe), but geologists took the position that at last the real truth had been found. When Darwin put forward his evolutionary hypothesis, it did not account for many of the facts as convincingly as the former idea of creation. But again, scientists largely took the position that at last the real truth had been found.

Copernicus' idea was taken up enthusiastically by Galileo Galilei. Galileo taught that it was an established, proven fact that the Universe is heliocentric (sun centred). Galileo got into trouble with the Inquisition.

The Inquisition was set up primarily to persecute Bible believers who Refused to accept the teachings of the established Church. In its disgraceful history it tortured and killed many Christians and many Jews, but it also persecuted a few philosophers and scientists, notable among them being Giordano Bruno and Galileo.

Illustration 44

Galileo Galilei

The reasons for Galileo's being in trouble with the members of the "Holy Office" are not usually mentioned. It was partly jealousy and opposition from the scientific establishment which saw the Inquisition as being able to remove someone whose hard work, clear thinking and inventiveness were an embarrassment to their own mindless repetition of Aristotle's speculations. It was also partly due to his lack of sensitivity in riding roughshod over other peoples feelings. He angered the pope by writing a book defending Copernicus in which he put the pope's words into the mouth of a dim-wit, "Simplicio", while himself giving clever arguments for heliocentricity. One of the things his enemies seized upon was his claim that the sun is at the centre of the universe. They pointed out that the Bible clearly puts the earth at the centre. The Inquisition demanded proof for his claim that the sun, instead, has that favoured position. He did not have any proof. He had observations which refuted Aristottle's crystal spheres, observations which refuted ancient arguments as to why the sun could not be the centre. And an utterly indefensible "proof" of heliocentricity based on the tides. He had earlier been given permission to teach heliocentricity as a useful theory, but not as an established fact. He continued to teach heliocentricity as proven truth, and ended up under house arrest in his comfortable villa. Copernicus's idea was not the only model proposed to replace that of Ptolemy.

Tycho Brahe is recognised as one of the greatest observational astronomers of all time. He spent most of his working life making the most accurate series

Illustration 45

Tycho Brahe

of astronomical observations that had ever been made. He recorded the positions of the sun, the moon, the planets and the stars. He devised a different model to explain his observations.

In Brahe's view the earth was stationary at the Centre of the universe. He was confident that was where both scripture and his observations showed it to be.

Brahe considered the moon to be orbiting the earth, the sun to be orbiting the earth, but the planets to be orbiting the sun. In this model the sun carries the planets around with it in the same way that Jupiter carries its moons with it as it orbits the sun. Brahe could satisfactorily account for his observations using this model.

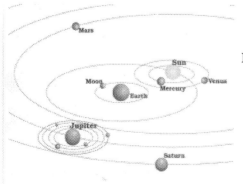

Illustration 46

Brahe's System

Brahe died before he could publish his findings. He left all his observations to his assistant, Johannes Kepler. Kepler promised to write up Brahe's observations in terms of his geocentric model. But Kepler only partially kept his promise. He described Brahe's model, and showed that all the observations are consistent with it, but he personally preferred Copernicus' model, and came out openly in support of heliocentricity.

Illustration 47

Johannes Kepler

Somewhat later he modified Copernicus' model. He kept the sun stationary at the centre of the universe, but he showed that observations were in better agreement with the idea that the planets move around the sun not in circles but in ellipses. He even "doctored" his observations to make them fit that scheme more convincingly. The idea of elliptical orbits received a tremendous boost when perhaps the greatest scientist of all time, Sir Isaac Newton, published his famous treatise on the principles of mechanics.

Newton showed that if one ignores the rest of the universe and considers just two bodies, the easiest equations describing their relative motion are obtained if one is thought of as fixed and the other is considered to move around it. It does not matter which of the two is considered stationary, the same equations result. They show the trajectory of the moving body to be an ellipse. Newton was a

Illustration 48

Isaac Newton

very great scientist. He realised that although this gives the easiest equations it does not necessarily describe the true situation. He also pointed out that his theory of gravity, although useful in giving answers to many problems, could not actually be true. He suggested several possible alternatives, but was dissatisfied with all of them. He considered the best suggestion he had come across to be that of Nicolas Fatio De Duillier. His idea, which was later plagiarised by Gorge Louis Le Sage who popularised it, has now been transformed into the theory of "gravitons". Most of the scientists who have come after Newton have not had anything like his abilities. Few have realised what he was talking about.

The "two body problem" ellipse is not a "true" description of reality:- more realistically both bodies move around their common centre of gravity. To describe that situation takes much more difficult equations. The usefulness of Newton's analysis is that it gives relative positions and motions very easily and accurately. That is usually all that is required. It is easy to forget the fact that it gives no clue as to reality in any "absolute" sense.

Illustration 49
Two Body Dynamics

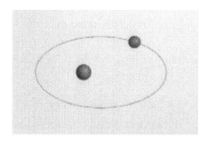

Newton showed that for the motion of just two bodies, the easiest equations are found if one ignores the rest of the universe and assumes one body to be at rest while the other moves around it. The moving body then describes an ellipse around the stationary body, which is at one focus of the ellipse.

Reality is not always described by the simplest equations.

The simplest equations do not necessarily describe reality.

When dealing with more than two bodies the easiest equations are found by taking the centre of gravity of all the bodies as stationary and considering their motion around this common centre. It does not matter whether the biggest body is at the centre, or the smallest, or no body at all.

It is presently believed by most astronomers that we are part of a galaxy called the "Milky Way". The Milky Way is widely believed to be a spiral with a "nucleus" containing thousands of millions of stars at its centre. Radiating from the centre are thought to be arms of stars, gas and dust which are being wound up into this spiral shape as the whole galaxy turns about its

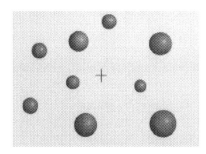

Illustration 50
Many Body Dynamics

The dynamics of more than two bodies is not so easy. One again ignores the rest of the universe and then considers the motion of each body around their common centre of gravity.

centre. It is thought that the sun is about two thirds of the way out from the centre. It is widely believed that the earth is hurtling around the sun at more than a hundred thousand kilometres per hour and that the solar system is speeding around the galaxy at about a million kilometres per hour.

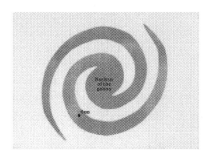

Illustration 51
The Milky Way
Most astronomers currently believe that the sun is about two thirds of the way from the centre of a spiral galaxy called the Milky Way. The sun is thought to be travelling round the galaxy at about a million kilometres per hour.

When dealing with the entire galaxy the easiest equations are found by taking the centre of gravity of the galaxy as stationary. Everything else (including our sun) is considered to move around it.

It is also believed that our galaxy is just one of a number in a group of galaxies called the "local cluster". Our galaxy is thought to be hurtling around the centre of gravity of the cluster at many millions of kilometres per hour. If we are dealing with the entire cluster, then the easiest equations occur when we take the centre of gravity of the cluster as stationary.

Clearly what is considered to be stationary depends on how much of the universe is being dealt with.

But if we were to consider the entire universe would it be unreasonable to ask whether there is some point, perhaps in some way the real the centre of gravity of the entire universe, which is truly stationary?

And if there is such a point would it be unreasonable to put forward the earth as a candidate for being in that position?

One of the greatest scientists of the 19th century was Ernst Mach[3]. He said:- "Obviously it matters little if we think of the earth as turning about on its axis, or if we view it at rest while the fixed stars revolve around it. Geometrically these are exactly the same case of a relative rotation of the earth and the fixed stars with respect to one another". Mach was, in fact, rather troubled by the fact that there is no sound reason, based on observation, to reject the idea that the earth could be stationary at the centre of the universe.

Fred Hoyle was one of the great scientists of the last century. According to him[4]:- "We know that the difference between a heliocentric theory and a geocentric theory is one of relative motion only, and that such a difference has no physical significance". So we see that Fred Hoyle has no fundamental objection to the possibility that the earth could be the centre of the universe either.

Are there any objections?

A red herring in the form of "the solar system" is often thrown in to muddy the waters. It is a theoretical construction thought up only in fairly recent times and has nothing to do with the question at hand. It is clear that the earth is not at the centre of this hypothetical system, but we are considering the reality of the entire universe, not a hypothetical sub-division of it.

There have been surprisingly few objections to the possibility of the earth being the centre of the universe; and each of them has been shown to be invalid. The observations would be the same whether the earth were stationary at the centre or not. Perhaps the most interesting of the objections is the aberration of starlight.

Bradley, the British Astronomer Royal, discovered that a star was never observed to be in its average position. He observed particularly the star "Gamma Draconis". His measurements throughout the year showed that its actual position moved around its average position in a tiny ellipse, completing one

3   Mach, E., DIE MECHANIK IN IHRER ENTWICKLUNG HISTORISCH-KRITISCH DARGESTELLT, 1883.

4   Hoyle, Sir F., ASTRONOMY AND COSMOLOGY — A MODERN COURSE, W.H. Freedman, p. 416.

circuit each year. He came to the conviction that this was the long awaited proof that the earth went round the sun. Science had long accepted heliocentricity, but up to that time no proof had ever been put forward. Bradley considered that here, at last, was proof.

To see why he took his "aberration ellipse" as evidence for heliocentricity consider a telescope pointing straight at a star. A beam of light coming from the star strikes exactly in the very centre of the objective lens. But the earth is moving, and the telescope is moving along with the earth. By the time the light reaches the eyepiece, the telescope will have moved slightly. Not very much, but because the speed of light is not infinite it has moved a little. So although the light came in absolutely in the centre at the top, it is not quite in the centre at the bottom — the light is left behind, The direction in which it is left behind depends on the direction that the earth is moving, and since the earth moves in an ellipse round the sun each year, the star will appear to trace out a little ellipse at the eyepiece.

Although Bradley (and many others) considered this proof that the earth really does go round the sun, there were some who noted that this need not be so. If Brahe had been right, and the sun orbited the earth, and if it carried everything else (including the stars) around with it, then the stars would actually be moving in ellipses around the earth once each year. The "aberration ellipse" would not be proof that the earth orbits the sun, but would simply be a result of the actual motion of the stars.

The coveted indisputable proof of heliocentricity seemed as elusive as ever, until a scientist called Ruggiero Boscovich proposed an experiment. Boscovich (who actually favoured Copernicus) suggested that a telescope be filled with water. The reason for proposing that is because light travels one and a half times slower in water than in air. Light would take one and a half times longer to reach the eyepiece, and the telescope would move one and a half times further in that time, so the aberration ellipse would be one and a half times bigger. But if the earth were stationary, and the ellipse were due to actual motion of the stars, then there would be no difference, the ellipse would be the same size. Here was a chance to prove, once and for all, apparently, whether the earth orbited the sun or not.

No one bothered to do the experiment. Scientists were so confident that the earth goes round the sun, and considered the idea that the earth is stationary so foolish, that they thought proof unnecessary.

But a scientist called Arago did experiments in which he put a plate of glass below his telescope. He found that when he moved the plate of glass, starlight was dragged along with it. Calculations showed that the observations agreed with the idea that the earth was stationary, but disagreed with the idea that it moves.[5] The British Astronomer Royal, George Bidel Airy[6], decided that someone ought to do Boscovich's experiment after all. He filled a telescope with water, and started observing.

It is interesting to remember that this experiment was specifically set up to test between two theories. If the earth is moving, then the ellipse ought to be one and a half times bigger, but if it is the stars which are moving, then the ellipse should be the same size. Airy did the experiment. He found, to his surprise, that the ellipse was exactly the same size.

Airy had just shown that the earth does not go round the sun.

As is normal in science, when experimental evidence runs counter to cherished ideas, ideas which affect the favoured world view, an ad hoc saved the theory from the evidence.

The ad hoc was a modification of an idea put forward by a well-known French scientist called Fresnel.

Fresnel did experiments in which he passed light through moving liquids and moving transparent solids. He found that the light was dragged along with the moving body or the moving liquid. He suggested that this was because the aether, the medium through which light travels, was being dragged along. Fresnel (and several other scientists) performed experiments to measure the properties of this aether.

The reason for proposing an aether is that all known wave forms need a medium to travel through. For example sound travels from a speaker's mouth to a listener's ear by pressure waves in the air. The air is the medium through which the sound waves travel. It had long been recognised that light has a wave form. It was realised that there must be some medium through which it travelled. This medium was given the name "Luminiferous Aether", or just "Aether" for short.

---

5   Arago F. 1839. COMPTES RENDUS, 8, 326

6   Airy, G.B., 1871. PROCEEDINGS OF THE ROYAL SOCIETY OF LONDON no.18, p. 12

To explain away Airy's failure "Fresnel drag" was put forward as the cause. As the earth hurtles through space it partially drags along the aether with it. If the aether were dragged along at just the right rate, then the ellipse in Airy's telescope could end up just the right size.

This explanation requires, of course that there is an aether, and it needs the aether to be dragged along at a very specific rate.

Having accepted this idea to explain away the only experiment yet devised to prove the motion of the earth, the scientists seemed to be left with no genuine method of finding out whether the earth was actually moving or not. Mechanically it seemed there was only the possibility of detecting relative motion, never absolute motion.

And that situation held until James Clarke Maxwell appeared on the scene.

James Clark Maxwell was one of the greatest physicists of the 19th century. He brought together all the known facts, all the known theories, all the known observations on electricity and magnetism and came up with his famous equations, "Maxwell's equations". He showed that moving electric charges generate magnetic fields, and that light is an electromagnetic phenomenon which has a fundamental constant speed through the aether (the aether being a fundamental aspect of his theory).

That threw a whole new light on the situation. As Professor Herbert Dingle pointed out "It was quite otherwise in electromagnetism. An electric charge

Illustration 52
James Clark Maxwell

Maxwell unified the physics of electricity and magnetism by his famous equations of electromagnetism. Radiation such as light consists of energy which constantly switches between electric and magnetic waves by reaction with the aether. His theory predicted radio waves, X-rays, microwaves, etc. which were soon discovered and put to good use.

at rest was surrounded only by an electric field, but an electric charge in motion was equivalent to an electric current and was surrounded by a magnetic field also".[7] So here was a method of detecting absolute rest and absolute motion. All that is needed is to look at an electric charge. If there is no magnetic field associated with it then the charge must be at rest, if there is a magnetic field, the strength of the magnetic field gives a measure of the absolute speed. Maxwell's result concerning light's constant speed through the aether meant that light could also be used to detect absolute motion.

Albert Abraham Michelson, a famous scientist who spent most of his professional career dealing with the speed of light, together with a colleague, Edward Williams Morley, designed and built an apparatus, an "interferometer", to measure the absolute motion of the earth through space. A description of the experiment and also the "interference fringes" and "fringe shifts" used in the method, can be found in most general physics textbooks.

Illustration 53
Albert Abraham Michelson

Michelson was one of the outstanding physicists of the late 19th and early 20th Centuries. Together with E.W. Morley he built an apparatus known as a "Michelson and Morley Interferometer" to measure the speed of the Earth through space. Their measurements indicated that the earth is not orbiting the sun.

A phenomenon called "interference" produces alternate light and dark bands called "interference fringes" or just "fringes" for short. The spacing of the fringes depends on the speed at which light strikes the apparatus. A change in the speed at which light strikes the equipment leads to a change in the spacing called a "fringe shift".

7 Dingle, Herbert; SCIENCE AT THE CROSSROADS, Martin Brian & O'Keefe, 1972 pp. 147–148

Michelson and Morley[8] planned to turn their apparatus until they found the maximum fringe shift produced by light travelling in two perpendicular directions. The position of maximum fringe shift would show the direction in which the earth was moving, the size of the fringe shift would be a measure of the speed of the earth through the aether.

But they found that no matter how they turned their apparatus, there was no significant fringe shift. They had once again established that the earth does not move. They reasoned that the movements of the earth around the sun, and the sun around the universe must have exactly cancelled out, so that just at that moment the earth happened to be stationary. The obvious thing to do was to repeat the experiment six months later, when the earth would be going in the opposite direction, on the "other side" of its orbit around the sun, and the motions would no longer cancel.

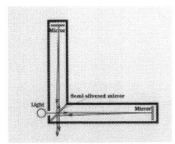

Illustration 54
Michelson and Morley Interferometer
If the Earth is moving through the aether, then light should take slightly longer to go back and forth in the arm of the apparatus which is pointing in the direction of motion than in the arm perpendicular to the motion. Whichever way they turned the apparatus there was no significant difference.

Illustration 55
Fringe Shifts
The spacing of fringes depends on the speed at which light strikes the apparatus. A decrease in speed would lead to the spacing being increased. Michelson and Morley expected that they would discover the direction of the Earth's motion by noting the direction of greatest fringe shift, and the absolute speed of this motion by the size of the shift.

8 Michelson, A.A., & Morley, E.W., AMERICAN JOURNAL OF SCIENCE; 1887, Vol 34

So they repeated the experiment six months later, but still there were no significant fringe shifts. The earth was still standing still! They repeated the experiment at all seasons of the year. They repeated it at all times of the day and night. They repeated it in Berlin, in Chicago, on the tops of mountains … and everywhere … no fringe shift.

In other words, the earth was not moving.

It is interesting to see what various scientists have said about this:-

Adolf Baker[9] said "Thus failure to observe different speeds of light at different times of the year suggested that the earth must be 'at rest' … it was therefore the 'preferred' frame for measuring absolute motion in space".

Bernard Jaffe[10] said "The data were almost unbelievable. There was only one other possible conclusion to draw, that the earth was at rest. This, of course, was preposterous".

But we might ask "Why preposterous?" After all, has anybody ever actually proved that the earth is moving?

Giancoli[11] put it this way:- "But this implies that the earth is somehow a preferred object; only with respect to the earth would the speed of light be c as predicted by Maxwell's equations. This is tantamount to assuming that the earth is the central body of the universe".

That of course is unacceptable to anyone who has decided that the earth is a very ordinary second class planet speeding through some insignificant backwater of the universe. Another ad hoc was required to save the theory from the evidence.

The man who came up with the germ of the idea for the required ad hoc was an Irish physicist called George Francis Fitzgerald. His suggestion was developed into the idea that if Michelson and Morley's apparatus contracted in the direction of the earth's motion, then, provided that the contraction was

---

9 Baker, Adolf, MODERN PHYSICS AND ANTIPHYSICS, Addison-Wesley, 1970 p. 54

10 Jaffe, Bernard, MICHELSON AND THE SPEED OF LIGHT, Doubleday, 1960 p. 76

11 Giancoli, Douglas, PHYSICS: PRINCIPLES WITH APPLICATIONS, Prentice-Hall, 1980 p. 625

just the right amount, no fringe shift would be observed. This contraction must occur with any moving body, which means that when one drives one's car (or one's spaceship) at high speed it becomes slightly shorter than when it was stationary. An interesting idea. To accept such an idea as scientific one should, of course, take measurements and check that it is so. Our intrepid motorist (or space traveller) takes his ruler with him and measures his vehicle to see if it really does become shorter. Unfortunately the ruler must get shorter by exactly the right amount to make the measurement identical to that when it is stationary.

Measurement says it does not get shorter.

Then how do we know it really does get shorter?

Obviously it must get shorter.

Otherwise Michelson and Morley's experiment shows that the earth stands still.

But there is a way to test for "Fitzgerald contraction". An interferometer would get shorter by exactly the right amount only if the lengths of the two arms were exactly equal. But if an interferometer were made with, say, one arm only half the length of the other, the contraction would no longer be just right, and a fringe shift would be observed. Such an interferometer was built. It is interesting to see Arthur Beiser's comment on this experiment:- "We might be tempted to consider the Michelson-Morley result solely as evidence for the contraction of the length of their apparatus in the direction of the earth's motion. This interpretation was tested by Kennedy and Thorndike using an interferometer with arms of unequal length. They also found no fringe shift, which means that these experiments must be considered evidence for the absence of an aether".[12]

But why "MUST be considered evidence for the absence of an aether"? Why not taken as evidence that the earth stands still? All the observations would fit that idea! And if this experiment proves that there is no aether, then it raises a very interesting philosophical question. Is it possible for scientists to measure properties of something that does not exist? Fresnel had measured properties of the aether. If it is possible for scientists to measure the properties of something that does not exist, then what value can we assign to science?

---

12 Beise, Arthur, PERSPECTIVES OF MODERN PHYSICS,McGraw-Hill 1983, p16

Anything the scientists measure might be a measurement of something that does not exist at all! But if it is not possible to measure properties of something that does not exist, then what about Fresnel's (and several other scientists') measurements of properties of the aether? And if there is no aether, how do we explain away the failure of Airy to find the result he expected in Boscovich's experiment? And how do we make sense of Maxwell's equations, which come directly from consideration of the aether?

It is intriguing to note that all the experiments fit in with the idea that the earth does not move … without the need for any ad hocs at all.

It was not only optical experiments that were giving this problem. Electromagnetic experiments, such as that of Trouton and Noble[13], also suggested that the earth does not move.

The man who came up with the way out of the dilemma was Hendrik Antoon Lorentz, a famous Dutch physicist. He proposed that high speed motion through the aether led not only to length contraction but also to increased resistance to acceleration (which is equivalent to increase in mass), and the slowing down of clocks. The famous "Lorentz Transformations" formed the core of his "Theory of Relativity".

A young genius working in the Swiss patent office, Albert Einstein, later expressed Lorentz's theory in a different way — as a mathematical abstraction without a physical basis. Expressed this way the theory needed no aether, in fact it could not tolerate the aether. It was later realised that this solved the problem of Thorndike and Kennedy's experiment. Einstein's version of relativity became more popular than Lorentz's, and the idea of the aether went out of fashion.[14]

Einstein's original contribution to relativity centres on two fundamental assumptions, neither of which is obvious, and both of which contradict Maxwell's

---

13   Trouton JF.T., and Noble, H.R., PROCEEDINGS OF THE ROYAL SOCIETY, 1903, Vol.72 p. 132

14   Most physicists continue to deny the existence of the aether, yet they are forced to admit that "free space" is, as K.W. Ford expressed it, "a turbulent sea of randomly fluctuating electromagnetic fields, and short-lived, virtual particle pairs that form and annihilate". It is generally agreed that key "vacuum" properties include intrinsic energy, permittivity, permeability and intrinsic impedance — properties associated with the "aether" of Maxwell and Lorentz. This gives the impression that its existence is denied in chosen circumstances simply by repudiating its former name.

Illustration 56
Antoon Lorentz

Lorentz proposed that high speed motion through the aether led to length contraction, increased resistance to acceleration and time dilation. He developed the "Theory of Relativity". Einstein later changed the theory to get rid of the aether.

equations (which the theory was intended to justify!). The first assumption is that no matter how an observer is (uniformly) moving he will always come to the same conclusion about the laws of science. No matter how he is moving he will always come to the same conclusions about the universe. In other words, all frames of reference are absolutely equivalent. The second assumption is that however an observer is (uniformly) moving, he will always measure the speed at which light reaches him as being the same, a constant, "c". This means that if the earth is moving through space with a speed "v", and it meets a ray of light moving in exactly the opposite direction in a head-on collision, then the impact speed will be c+v but this will be exactly equal to c! A ray of light moving in the same direction as the earth, catching the earth up, will meet the earth with an impact speed of c-v, and this will also be exactly equal to c.

So $(c + v) = c = (c - v)$

To anyone with a little knowledge of mathematics it looks as if there is one, unique, solution, $v = 0$ … the earth is not moving.

But according to Einstein it is true for any value of v!

So $c + c/2 = c = c - c/2$!

When a relativity teacher (or a textbook) presents this to a reasonably intelligent student, it is, of course, greeted with incredulity. But the teacher says:- "Assume that this is true for the moment, then we will develop the theory. We will see that it makes a number of predictions. And then we'll look at experiments which have been done. We will see that the experimental results agree with the theory, and that will prove that this assumption was true after all".

But what our student is not told is that most of the experiments confirm

Lorentz's theory which was in existence before Einstein's version of relativity. Others agree equally well, or better, with theories other than Relativity (often simpler and more reasonable). Students are often told, for example, that the atomic bomb is a wonderful proof of relativity, because "e = m.c²" was predicted by relativity. What they are not told is that Poincare derived e=m.c² long before Einstein. Nor are they told that it can be deduced from considerations having nothing to do with relativity in one or two lines of very simple mathematics.[15]

Most scientists accepted relativity joyfully. By abandoning physical reasoning, and accepting pure mathematical formalism, it gave them a plausible excuse to ignore all the evidence that the earth is stationary. Part of their acceptance required rejecting the existence of the aether. But a French scientist called Sagnac seemed unconvinced. No one had ever proved that the earth was actually moving, and Relativity was based on the assumption that it must be moving. In fact Relativity is largely an ad hoc to explain away the observations that show the earth to be stationary at the centre of the universe (Einstein's denial notwithstanding!).

Sagnac[16] built a turn-table with mirrors on it arranged in such a way that a beam of light was split into two beams, one was reflected from mirror to mirror anticlockwise around the turntable, the other was reflected around clockwise. After a complete circuit the beams were recombined in a camera to give interference fringes. Looking at it in a very simplified way, when the turntable was set spinning there was known to be movement, the beam going round with the turn table's rotation would be chasing the camera (which is moving away at speed v) with a relative speed of c-v, whereas the beam going against the rotation would approach the camera "head on" with a relative speed of c+v. If the basic assumptions of Relativity were correct, with c+v = c-v, and no aether, then there should be no fringe shift.

But there was a fringe shift. A basic assumption of Relativity was apparently wrong. More explanations were needed to keep Relativity and the motion of the earth alive. But the excuses of the relativists were tested, experimentally and theoretically, and found to be invalid. Eventually the famous physicist

---

15   Aspden H., MODERN AETHER SCIENCE, Sabberton Publications, 1972

16 Sagnac, G., COMPTES RENDUS, 157, 708 & 1410

17 Ives, Herbert E., JOURNAL OF THE OPTICAL SOCIETY OF AMERICA., 1938, Vol.28 pp. 296–299

Herbert Ives[17] pointed out that the only way to carry on believing in Relativity was to "avoid looking at" the evidence. Arguments are still being put forward to explain away Sagnac's experiment. Interestingly enough there are a number of explanations of such problems for Einstein's "Special Theory of Relativity" (STR) which appeal to his "General Theory of Relativity" (GTR). Now STR cannot have an aether and must have a constant velocity of light. On the other hand GTR is, as Einstein put it "unthinkable without the aether" and cannot tolerate a constant velocity of light. The two theories are mutually exclusive. At least one must be wrong. To solve difficulties for one by calling in the other is clearly invalid.

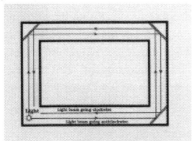

Illustration 57
Michelson and Gale Experiment

Rotation of the Earth should carry the southern section of the apparatus (which is closer to the equator), more quickly through a stationary aether than the northern section. Light travelling from West to East should be slowed down because of moving "against" the aether, light moving from East to West should be speeded up because of moving "'with" the aether. Light travelling clockwise around the tunnel should be "speeded up" in the southern section more than it is "slowed down" in the northern section:- the opposite will happen to light travelling anticlockwise. The clockwise beam should take less time for a complete circuit. Michelson and Gale found that this is actually so.

Michelson, together with a new collaborator called Gale[18], thought of a way to test whether the aether exists or not.

They built a tunnel of pipe sections at Chicago. The tunnel was in the form of a large rectangle. They reasoned that if there were an aether, then the rotation of the earth from west to east through it should cause a beam of light travelling clockwise round the tunnel to take slightly less time to get round than a beam travelling anticlockwise. If there were no aether then both beams would take the same time.

They measured a difference. Existence of aether established. Einstein certainly made some brilliant contributions to science, but his modification of Lorentz's theory of relativity was evidently wrong again. Explanations have, of course, been thought up!

Michelson and Gale took their observations as clear proof that there is an aether. They also took it as clear proof that the earth is rotating through this aether. But it has been pointed out that it is not actually a complete proof of the earth's rotation. The same result would be observed if the earth were rotating and the aether were standing still, or if the earth were standing still with the universe, including the aether rotating around it, or if the earth were partially rotating and the aether were partially rotating. But it certainly does seem to establish that there is, indeed, a relative rotation between the earth and the aether.

An intriguing point to note about this is that although several "proofs" have been put forward that the earth must rotate on its axis, all appear to be invalid. The Foucault pendulum, the earth's equatorial bulge, geo-stationary satellites and other phenomena have all been put forward by scientists who have not understood what Ernst Mach was talking about when he pointed to the crucial role of the "fixed stars". Einstein, in his fundamental paper on General Relativity[19] showed that he certainly understood. He noted that if relativity, even in the form put forward by Newton, were to hold, then if the earth did not rotate, the universe rotating around it would have to generate a field which would produce exactly equivalent forces. Hans Thirring demonstrated this explicitly by deriving the form of the field generated by the rotation of matter analogous to the rotation of the stars around the earth.[20] He showed that the field due to a rotating shell of material leads to centrifugal force and coriolis force as real forces whereas in Newtonian mechanics they are fictitious — the apparent result of accelerations. Astounding as it may seem there is no experiment yet devised by science which has established whether the earth actually rotates or not.

19 Einstein A. Berl. Ber. 1914, S.1030

20 Thirring H., PHYSIKALISCHE ZEITSCHRIFT, 19:33–39, 1. Feb. 1918

The experiments of Sagnac and Michelson & Gale are rarely mentioned. Until recently it was quite difficult to find a reference to them. As Dean Turner[21] pointed out "One may scan Einstein's writings in vain to find mention of the Sagnac or Michelson-Gale experiments. The same can be said of general physics text-books and of the McGraw-Hill Encyclopaedia of Science and Technology ... Such an oversight constitutes a stinging indictment of professional scientific reporting". It is indeed quite difficult to get information on these experiments. They seem to be such an embarrassment to relativity that those who know about them would rather not say too much. Quite a number of relativity experts, however, do know about them, and when pressed many admit that they show the Special Theory of Relativity (the theory taught to all science students, and the basis for much of "modern physics") to be inadequate. Some point out that the difficulties can be explained away by working in terms of "Riemanian space", a mathematical abstraction which can be bent, warped and twisted in as many dimensions as a mathematician may care to invent. Since the reality which we live in actually seems to consist of normal ("Euclidian") space of exactly three dimensions which are "flat" (i.e. not bent, warped or twisted) these arguments are only convincing to confirmed believers in Einstein's theory — or to those so intimidated by the mathematics that they are afraid to appear ignorant if they disagree!

It was not only experiments like those of Sagnac and Michelson and Gale which pointed to the earth as central. Edwin Hubble discovered that the fainter a galaxy appeared in his telescope (and therefore presumably the further away), the more its spectrum was shifted to the red. It did not matter in which direction he looked. In every direction, the further away from the earth the more "red shifted" the spectrum. This is usually explained in terms of what is called the "Doppler" effect. The "redder" the spectrum, the faster something is supposed to be moving away from us. This leads to the idea of the "expanding universe". The further an object is from us, the faster it is moving away from us. It is almost certain that this interpretation is wrong. Scientists like Halton Arp and W.G. Tift[22] have shown that the red shifts are probably not due to the Doppler Effect and the universe may not be expanding at all. But whatever the explanation, the earth is clearly at the centre of whatever is causing these red shifts.

---

21 Turner, Dean, THE EINSTEIN MYTH AND THE IVES PAPERS, Devin-Adair, 1979 p. 44

22 Arp, H., ASTRONOMY, 1978, Vol.6 p. 15. Tift W.G., ASTROPHYSICAL JOURNAL, 1991, 382: 396–415; Arp. H.; Seeing Red; Judaica Press; NY, 1996, ISBN 1-880582-24-4)

Bent, twisted and warped Riemanian geometry can again explain this away to believers in the General Theory of Relativity. It explains that the universe is a figure with its centre everywhere and its circumference nowhere. For those with the ability to imagine such a figure (or the willingness to believe in it without being able to imagine it!) it implies that no matter where one finds oneself in the universe, one will always think one is at the centre, and one's observations will always fit that idea.

At the beginning of the last century the Dutch astronomer Jacobus Kapteyn hit upon the idea of counting the stars in pairs of opposite directions. His counts indicated that we are in the centre — he found the same number of stars in each pair of opposite directions. But to get over this observation that we are at the centre a good explanation was at hand — clouds of gas and dust must hide the stars which would unbalance the star counts!

Astronomers did a survey of the distribution of the mass in the universe. The material in the universe is actually distributed rather unevenly, it is what is called a "lumpy" distribution. It is so lumpy that it is a serious embarrassment to the Big-Bang theory. But in spite of its lumpiness the mass in the universe does, on the whole, seem to lie in a pattern. The pattern comprises concentric shells centred on the earth. The earth seems to be in the centre of the densest part of the universe[23]. Most scientists do not like that, it is not popular to have the earth at the centre of anything, especially since these observations were not easy to explain away — even with the help of bent, twisted and warped Riemanian mathematics. A "dimming factor" was applied. It was then expected that the figures would show a uniform distribution of matter throughout the universe. But it was found that the earth is still at the centre of concentric shells, the earth being now in the least dense part of the universe.

In 1990 a report[24] came up in the scientific world about "mega-walls" across the cosmos. In "Science Frontiers"[25] the editor commented:- "wouldn't it be hilarious if the earth were at the centre of these concentric shells. … some measurements of the universe's rotation also seem to imply geocentrism".

23 Slusher, H.S., THE ORIGIN OF THE UNIVERSE, I.C.R. Technical monograph. pp. 12–13

24 Henbest, Nigel, *Galaxies Form Megawalls Across Space*, NEW SCIENTIST, 1990, 990, p. 37

25 Corliss W., SCIENCE FRONTIERS, 1990, No.69

The mega-walls were soon confirmed to be concentric shells centred on the earth.[26]

Evidence that the earth is at the centre of the universe seems to be the rule rather than the exception.

Quasars are a mystery. Nobody knows what they are, but scientists have done a lot of work on them. It has been found that the various classes of quasar lie on concentric shells centred on the earth. In one of Astronomy's most respected journals Varshni[27] had this to say:- "The cosmological interpretation of the red shift in the spectra of quasars leads to yet another paradoxical result, namely that the earth is the centre of the universe".

Varshni, being a good scientist, was not prepared to accept evidence which showed the earth to be at the centre of anything. He proposed an ad hoc to explain the evidence away.

But we might ask why the scientists always need to invent excuses to explain away the evidence? Is it not possible that the earth really is stationary at the centre of the universe? Why the unwillingness to consider that possibility?

Rutherford[28] probably came close to answering that question when he said:- "Even if it is recognised that different frames of reference are possible mathematically, a reference system that is acceptable to one person may involve PHILOSOPHICAL ASSUMPTIONS that are unacceptable to another". Now doesn't that ring a bell? Why did Copernicus take the earth away from the centre in the first place? The philosophical assumptions of his Greek mentors.

Burgess, writing in "Earth Chauvinism" probably came even closer to the truth when he said this:- "The story of Christianity tells about a plan of salvation centred upon a particular people and a particular man. As long as someone is thinking in terms of a geocentric universe the story has a certain plausibility. As soon as astronomy changes theories, however, the whole Christian history loses the only setting within which it would make sense. With the solar system no longer the centre of anything, imagining that what happens

---

26 Koo D., Szalay A., Kron R., Munn J., *A Universe of Bubbles and Voids*, SKY AND TELESCOPE, Sept 1990, p. 239

27 Varshni, Y.P., ASTROPHYSICS AND SPACE SCIENCE, 1976, Vol.43, p. 3

28 Rutherford, James F., et. al. THE PROJECT PHYSICS COURSE, Rinehart and Winston, 1970. Unit 2 p. 40

here forms the centre of a universal drama becomes simply silly". The secular humanist is not very eager to lend plausibility to the Christian story. As Professor J.E. Henry pointed out in "Geocentrism and Heliocentrism":- "The possibility that we have a special place in the universe is depressing to the humanist and is to be absolutely avoided". Another point to note is that most scientists are afraid for their reputation, they know that if they oppose the beliefs of the powerful establishment of science, they will incur ridicule and rejection. The famous physicist Alexander von Humboldt realised this when he said[29] "I have known, too, for a long time, that we have no arguments for the Copernican system, but I shall never dare to first attack it. Don't rush into the wasp's nest. You will bring upon yourself the scorn of the thoughtless multitude. If once a famous astronomer arises against the present conception, I will communicate, too, my observations; but to come forth as the first against opinions which the world has become fond of — I don't feel the courage".

Well, what then is the real situation? Where in the universe are we? Is it true that we are lost in some forgotten corner of the universe like a grain of sand in the Sahara Desert? Secular humanists love to say "Even if there were a God, he would never be able to find us". But is there actually any indisputable proof?

Is it possible that we could be at the centre of some great universal drama? Is there any indisputable disproof?

And does it actually matter? Does it really make any difference?

Astronomically it makes a huge difference. According to the Copernican principle we are an ordinary planet circling an ordinary star in some ordinary place in the universe. In that case we can be pretty sure that the laws of nature observed here will be the same as they are in the rest of the universe.

If Newton's laws hold here they must surely hold everywhere. If the speed of light here is 300 000 km per second here then that must be its value elsewhere. If we observe patterns in astronomical data we can be certain that those patterns can be interpreted in terms of a uniform spread of stars, galaxies, and everything else in space.

If the earth is in any way "special" though, those assumptions would not be reasonable at all. It would mean that all the astronomers' theories could fall in

---

29 C.Schoeppfer, THE EARTH STANDS FAST, Chas. Ludwig, NY, 1900, p. 59.

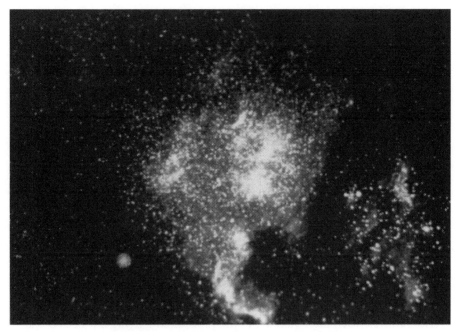

Illustration 58   North America Nebula
We have become accustomed to believing that objects like the North America
Nebula are collections of vast numbers of stars, which are assumed to be rather like
our sun, and millions of light years away. But no one actually knows what they are,
or how far away they really are. If the earth is in any way "special" then many of the
theories used to reach these conclusions may fall apart.

ruins and all their cosmological speculations could crumble.

Also, if we are going around the sun, then we have an orbit with a diameter of
about 300 million kilometres. That orbit can be used to deduce the distances
to the nearest stars, which, after making some fairly reasonable assumptions,
turn out to be about four and a half light years away. Building up from there,
using more assumptions, guesses and untested theories, we come to the
conclusion that the universe is at least twenty thousand million light years in
diameter.

If the earth stands still, we do not have that base-line of three hundred million
kilometres. The same observations could lead to a completely different conclusion. Assumptions made assuming the Copernican principle are no-longer
reasonable. Making some other fairly reasonable assumptions one can con-

clude that the furthest objects in the universe may be only about sixty light days away. Which means that the total diameter of the universe would be about one hundred and twenty light days. Different assumptions about how the stars move and how the aether behaves would lead to different distances … giving a greater — or perhaps, even, a smaller size.

This is very significant because the distances affect all our ideas about what the astronomical bodies actually are. An astronomer sees a smudge of light on his photograph. He interprets this as the image of a galaxy, and assigns a distance to it. He assumes that this galaxy is a group of stars. He assumes that the stars are very similar to our sun. He then reasons that the galaxy must consist of thousands of millions of stars in order to appear so bright at such a huge distance. If the distances are wrong then his conclusion will be wrong — in fact, the generally accepted ideas about most astronomical objects will be wrong. Scientifically it makes a huge difference. Clearly this question is of major significance.

Just how significant began to dawn on the scientists of NASA and Los Alamos Laboratories when their tracking of the Pioneer and Voyager probes began to show their spacecraft slowing down more quickly than they should if Newton's laws hold far from the earth.. The probes were sent in different directions but they all show that the further they get from us the more their behaviour disagrees with Newton's laws - which work just fine here on earth. There is even doubt that they will carry their information-packed gold discs out of the solar system. Those discs were intended for the alien civilisations they were supposed to reach sometime in the next two million years. But it looks as if they are slowing down so much that they will fall back towards the sun instead.

The Copernican principle seems a lot less certain than it did just a few years ago.

Where, then, in the universe are we?

A significant body of evidence seems to suggest it is not impossible that we could be at its centre.

Until certain scientists began claiming to have proved otherwise, all those who studied the Scriptures were convinced that is exactly where the Bible shows us to be.

Chapter 7

Are We Honest With Ourselves?

If civilization and society are to enjoy the fruits of moral uprightness — peace, harmony, progress and prosperity, the members of society must be, themselves, moral and committed to standards of honesty. Of all its representatives, scientists are expected to conform to the highest canon of integrity. This was clearly noted by Sir Henry Dale, an outstanding scientist of highest repute, when he wrote:- "And science, we should insist, better than any other discipline, can hold up to its students and followers an ideal of patient devotion to the search for objective truth, with vision unclouded by personal or political motive, not tolerating any lapse from precision or neglect of any anomaly, fearing only prejudice and preconception, accepting nature's answers humbly and with courage, and giving them to the world with an unflinching fidelity. The world cannot afford to lose such a contribution to the moral framework of its civilization".

This is the picture which most members of society seem to hold, but a glance at the situation existing today gives cause for doubt. As an example, Stephen Jay Gould, one of the world's most respected palaeontologists, noted:- "The extreme rarity of transitional forms in the fossil record persists as the trade secret of palaeontology ... We fancy ourselves as the only true students of life's history, yet to preserve our favoured account of evolution by natural selection we view our data as so bad that we never see the very process we profess to study".

Dale's portrayal of science has no place for "trade secrets", especially on such a subject as the theory of evolution, a theory which has profound influence in moulding the world view and moral foundation of the pupils and students of the world. To comply with Dale's picture would we not expect scientists to "humbly and with courage" tell the world "with unflinching fidelity" the fact that the students of evolution never see the process they profess to study, rather than keeping it a "trade secret"?

Several more secrets seem to exist in evolutionary "science". An alarming example is provided by Ernst Haeckel, a German biologist, who was not at all fainthearted when it came to inventing evidence for his theories — making up for the fact that actual evidence was lacking. One of his most famous inventions was the idea that a developing embryo goes through stages "recapitulating", or repeating, the process of evolution. It was very soon realised that this was not true, and Haeckel was brought before the senate of his university and accused of fraudulently altering his observations to fit his theory. Haeckel did not deny the obvious truth of the charges, but defended himself by saying that other scientists were guilty of the same offence. The story would not be very remarkable if that were the end of the affair. After all, deceptions do, unfortunately occur, but as long as they are uncovered and put right, then hopefully not too much harm should be done. Scientists are fully aware of Haeckel's fraud and also of the fact that it leads to wrong conclusions. Isaac Asimov, a devoted evolutionist, admitted:- "Haeckel used his principle (evolutionary recapitulation) to work up lines of evolutionary descent for various creatures and these lines are now known to be far wide of the mark". But amazingly, Haeckel's idea is still being taught as a demonstration of evolution! Eminent scientists have shown how utterly untenable the idea is, and yet school books, and even university textbooks, continue to use it as support for evolutionary thinking. Some even continue to state that a human embryo develops gill slits — an idea disproved almost as soon as Haeckel proposed it. The fact that evolutionary recapitulation has been totally discredited seems to be another trade secret which is being kept from the non-scientist rather than holding to the principle of "not tolerating any lapse from precision or neglect".

In evolutionary theory examples could readily be multiplied — the evolution of the horse, the protein molecular "clock", the story of "Vestigial organs", "homologous" structures, etc. In each case one finds that the ideas were presented to the world with loud acclamation, but when they were discovered to be wishful thinking or self deception, impressive public announcements were not made. Many people (including a large number of second-rate scientists) still sincerely believe some of these ideas, and have no idea that they have been totally discredited.

Dale's noble picture of science would expect the public admission of error

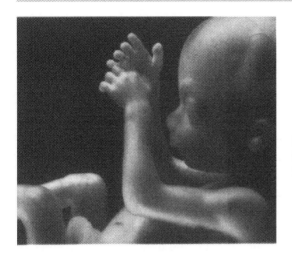

Illustration 59
Human Foetus

Ernst Haeckel popularised the story that an unborn baby follows evolutionary stages of development, and even has gill slits at an early phase. Although completely untrue it is still being taught as fact.

and "accepting nature's answers humbly and with courage, and giving them to the world with an unflinching fidelity". Although many scientists have admitted that the theory of evolution is completely untenable, most decline to make the fact public, some giving as their reason the possibility that society would lose confidence entirely in science and scientists.

It would certainly appear that the sciences concerned with biological evolution are not really being honest, either with themselves or with the public at large. But what about other branches of science? Astronomy is known as the "Queen Of The Sciences".

The famous astronomer Sir Arthur Edington noted:- "For the reader resolved to eschew theory and admit only definite observational facts, all astronomical books are banned. There are no purely observational facts about the heavenly bodies. Astronomical measurements are, without exception, measurements of phenomena occurring in a terrestrial observatory or station; it is only by theory that they are translated into knowledge of a universe outside".

Quite so. In principle the astronomer points his telescope at an object a great distance away. He lets the light coming down his telescope leave an impression on a photographic plate. He then tries to make sense of the spots and smudges of light on the photograph by theorizing about what the sources of light could be. In view of the very speculative nature of this, one would expect that all astronomers would acknowledge that their ideas about the heavenly bodies (except perhaps those which have actually been closely observed by space probes) are tentative postulations. This should be particularly evident, since every space probe which has been sent for a close examination of a heavenly body has shown that theories which the scientists had held about those bodies were utterly wrong in many respects. We would thus expect that as soon as one of their speculations had been shown to be false, it would be readily rejected.

That this is not, in fact, the case, can be seen in the explanation of the existence of short period comets in terms of Oort's cloud, as mentioned in Chapter 5. Despite the fact that papers like Lytelton's "The Non-Existence of the Oort Cometary Shell" have shown the idea to be wrong, it is still presented to the public almost as established fact. One is filled with wonder by Carl Sagan's statement:- "Many scientific papers are written each year about the Oort cloud — its origin, its properties, its evolution. Yet there is not a shred of observational evidence for its existence". Can a reasonable definition of science encompass a field in which belief in a speculation based on not one shred of evidence takes precedence over clear demonstration that the speculation is wrong?

It even happens that astronomers publish ideas that they know perfectly well cannot possibly be true at all. As an example, three respected American astronomers published an article in Nature[1], one of the most prestigious journals of science, in which they explained the partial disappearance of quasars over a period of several months. They proposed that clouds of various kinds of particles (which they called "Extreme Scattering Event Structures") moved into the line of sight and obscured the quasars. They proposed that there must be more of these structures in our galaxy than there are stars. Their paper was reviewed in another journal[2], where the well-known author commented, "The most intriguing thing about the hypothesised structures, a point the authors of the report hesitated to emphasise but did allude to, is that these objects are not stable … if such an object could exist, for even a moment, it would quickly dissipate".

In other words, the astronomers actually knew that such a structure could not exist for even one moment, and yet they told us there are thousands of millions of them in our galaxy. To someone fully believing that science still works as Dale described it, that may come as a surprise — but not to the scientists themselves. The reviewer continued "Like all good scientists, they are able to tolerate the ambiguities in their model".

---

1   Dennison, Fiedler & Johnston, NATURE, April 16, 1987

2   Gerrit L. Verschuur, ASTRONOMY, December 1987

How different from Dale's view of "patient devotion to the search for objective truth, with vision unclouded by personal or political motive, not tolerating any lapse from precision or neglect of any anomaly". Unfortunately today there are very specific personal motives which tend to cloud the vision of scientists. Not least of these is the "publish or perish" mentality, which links the status (and prospects for promotion) of a present-day scientist to the number, not the quality, or the honesty, of his publications.

Although astronomy should be recognised as a very speculative occupation, physics has the reputation of being the most exact of all the sciences. Here, at least we should expect to find the intellectual honesty portrayed in Dale's picture of science. Measurements and reason must surely point out errors and ensure the highest standards of integrity. The well-known physicist, Professor Herbert Dingle, an acknowledged expert on the theory of Relativity, long believed that this was indeed so. But his eyes were opened when his researches led him to a number of indications that Einstein's version of relativity could not be true. Dingle gave one particularly simple demonstration that it must be false. He showed that the theory requires that one clock must run steadily and continuously both faster and (at the same time) slower than another identical clock. To his amazement he found that science was not interested in having one of its favourite theories challenged.

His simple demonstration of the untenability of Einstein's theory was evaded, ridiculed, and eventually ignored. Dingle was certain that Einstein's version of relativity would eventually be disproved experimentally, and pointed out that it could be a highly dangerous experiment which gave the proof — perhaps one involving a nuclear chain reaction which could destroy a whole nation. As it turned out, this was not so, the experiments which have finally convinced open-minded scientists that Dingle was right and Einstein was wrong have concerned such things as the detailed behaviour of satellites — they do not behave as Einstein's theory says they should. But surprisingly few scientists seem to be open-minded enough to actually admit that Einstein could have been wrong. Many seem determined to uphold him at all costs.

The lengths to which some will go in this can be seen in a famous experiment by Hafele and Keating, who flew atomic clocks around the world in jet aircraft. Their results confirming Einstein's predictions were immediately published and received wide acclaim. The eminent physicist Louis Essen, who played a major part in the development of the atomic clock, examined their data and found that their results were simply a consequence of the choice of start and end times for the calibration of the clocks. In effect they chose a particular instant when one clock was "behind" the other as the start of their calibration period, and a judicious instant when it had "caught up" as its end. With a longer calibration period the results do not agree with Einstein at all.[3] Yet this experiment is cited in practically all modern physics textbooks as a conclusive proof of relativity.

As a contrast, when Dr. Silvertooth of Jet Propulsion Laboratories, Pasadena, California showed that orbiting atomic clocks used in the NAVSTAR project disprove Einstein's version of relativity no "respectable" journal would publish his results![4] Nor would they publish Essen's critique.

Many physicists continue their work as if experiment had not shown their sacrosanct theory to be in error, raising the possibility that the disaster Dingle feared might still happen!

The treatment meted out to Dingle when he presumed to point out flaws in an accepted theory of science reminds one of Humboldt's statement:- "I have known, too, for a long time, that we have no arguments for the Copernican system, but I shall never dare to first attack it. Don't rush into the wasp's nest. You will bring upon yourself the scorn of the thoughtless multitude. If once a famous astronomer arises against the present conception, I will communicate, too, my observations; but to come fourth as the first against opinions which the world has become fond of — I don't feel the courage".

This contrasts rather sharply with Dale's picture of scientists "with vision unclouded by personal or political motive, not tolerating any lapse from precision or neglect of any anomaly, fearing only prejudice and preconception, accepting nature's answers humbly and with courage"

A rather striking example of rather the opposite situation, prejudice and preconception not tolerating the admission of any anomaly, was given by the treatment of the scientific world to the discoveries of Immanuel Velikovsky, a medical man with archaeological interests. His training in psychology gave him a Freudian mind-set which rather coloured his interpretation of the data, yet nevertheless, the data itself deserved serious consideration, and showed, without any shadow of doubt, that several assumptions of accepted science, including the time scale, were in need of reconsideration. Not only that, but Velikovsky's theories led him to make some very specific predictions con-

---

3 Essen L., CRSQ, vol. 14, 1977, p. 96

4 Bouw G.D., WITH EVERY WIND OF DOCTRINE, Tychonian Society, 1984; p. 213.

trary to those of conventional scientific wisdom. His predictions later proved to be correct, and those of conventional science incorrect. But this did not lead to his data being taken seriously. Instead it led to a fresh crop of ad hocs justifying the old theories. Velikovsky was ridiculed, conspired against and suppressed to such an extent that some very distinguished members of the scientific profession acquired the title of "The Scientific Mafia" because of their treatment of him.[5]

But how did this situation come about? Why are things like this?

A common thread running through the examples noted above is that they all have a strong bearing on the tenability of the humanist world-view. A view which has gradually become so deeply entrenched in the last hundred years that it is now the requisite religion of science. Without the theory of evolution the humanist world view falls in ruins. Without the vast ages of uniformitarian geology and astronomy, evolution loses all semblance of credibility. Without relativity there is apparently no easy way out of accepting the evidence for the earth being a very special place. And that, as noted by Professor Henry, is a possibility which is "depressing to the humanist and to be absolutely avoided" — and also, as Humboldt noted, likely to bring a swarm of scientific wasps about one's ears.

Dale's precepts would lead to secular humanism being recognised as an unacceptable basis for science.

One might even wonder if Dale would recognise today's "scientists" as taking part in the same discipline he was talking about when he spoke of "their patient devotion to the search for objective truth". Today many have begun to claim that science does not seek such truth, but simply theories which explain observations in a satisfactory manner. One is tempted to suspect that this view is a result of the overthrow of many of the loud claims of humanist scientists which (after years of acceptance) have been shown to be false, and the refusal to contemplate the alternatives — which are philosophically unacceptable to the humanist world view.

In 1997 the famous Harvard professor Richard Lewontin made the astonishing statement:- "We take the side of science in spite of the patent absurdity of some of its constructs, in spite of its failure to fulfil many of its extravagant

---

5 Stove David, *The Scientific Mafia*, VELIKOVSKY RECONSIDERED, Sidgewick & Jackson, London, 1976

promises of health and life, in spite of the tolerance of the scientific community for unsubstantiated just-so stories, because we have a prior commitment, a commitment to materialism. It is not that the methods and institutions of science somehow compel us to accept a material explanation of the phenomenal world, but, on the contrary, that we are forced by our a-priori adherence to material causes to create an apparatus of investigation and a set of concepts that produce material explanations, no matter how counterintuitive, no matter how mystifying to the uninitiated. Moreover, that materialism is an absolute, for we cannot allow a Divine Foot in the door." [6]

It is hard to believe that Lewontin is talking about the same discipline as Dale.

Dale's last sentence:- "The world cannot afford to lose such a contribution to the moral framework of its civilization" has been left to go unheeded. And that raises the question:- to what extent has the decline in the moral framework of modern civilization — such a marked feature of the last few decades — been a direct consequence of scientists turning away from the principles which ought to guide their every step? To what extent are the swelling numbers of drug addicts victims of the theory of evolution's world view of life without purpose, of a chance existence without rhyme or reason. To what extent are today's soaring divorce rates, staggering crime figures and alarming AIDS statistics a product of a pointless world view which puts us as accidentally mutated amoebas on an insignificant chunk of rock swirling around in some forgotten corner of an incomprehensibly vast universe which is nothing more than the incidental product of an explosion anyway? A world view without responsibility, absolute values or moral standards.

But before we point a finger at the scientific establishment for its unwillingness to accept challenges in matters conflicting with prejudices and preconceived humanistic dogmas, perhaps we ought to ask ourselves personally the question:-

"Are we honest with ourselves?"

---

6   Richard Lewontin, The New York Review, Jan. 9, 1997, p.31

Chapter 8

What Can We Do About It?

It is clear that some of the most popular theories of speculative "science" are exerting an enormous influence on the whole of society. In many cases these influences have been undeniably detrimental. It is also clear that science has become a profession over which there is little or no external control. Despite impassioned denial by many scientists it is also a profession which has lost much of the integrity for which it was long famed. In particular there is little or no control (or self control) over the integrity of popular scientific reporting. Most scientists would be extremely unwilling to envisage any such control, and many people might be surprised at the suggestion that such control might be needed. But it should be noted that most professions submit themselves to codes of behaviour.

Engineers are subject to a code of practice which would, for example, prevent an engineer from designing a nuclear reactor unless he had adequate qualifications to do so. The medical profession has a code of conduct which covers for example, sexual molestation of patients. The legal profession's code covers such things as responsibility in the handling of clients' money.

The need for looking at the practice, and, more particularly, the reporting of science becomes clear when we see how profound its influence on society is. A good example is the theory of evolution. This theory has had enormous influence on world history. Karl Marx said that Charles Darwin had made "scientific socialism" possible. The communist experiment of Eastern Europe had its foundation in Darwin's theory of evolution, and in Marx's own estimation would have been impossible without it. Evolution has had a great influence on legal systems the world over. Considering man to be simply an accidentally enhanced wild animal leads to a particular view of his responsibilities in behaving like a human being rather than a beast. A view completely different to that held when man was believed to have been created by God.

Violent crime and its punishment have come to be widely judged on the understanding that man cannot be blamed too much for behaviour conditioned by bestiality in previous evolutionary states of existence. The influence of evolution on morality has been extreme. If man is simply the result of random chance processes, then his laws and moral standards are purely conventional. Society can choose its standards of good and bad, right or wrong to suit its circumstances. Absolute standards do not exist, and therefore there is no real reason why each person should not set his own standards. As a direct result of the acceptance of evolution every individual, or every government, has the right to decide on such questions as homosexuality, drug use, marital faithfulness, euthanasia and abortion.

And yet there has never been one experiment performed which has upheld the theory of evolution, either the evolution of life from non-life, or the evolution of one "kind" into another. Every mathematical analysis of the probability of evolution has shown it to be untenable. Vast numbers of observations contradict the theory. Great scientists have variously described the theory as "nonsense of a high order", "a fairy tale for grown-ups", "the greatest deceit in the history of science", and "a scientific religion".

The widespread acceptance of this totally unjustified hypothesis, and its enormous influence on society, and even the course of world history illustrates the power which scientists (and particularly dishonest reporters of science) wield.

It also illustrates an even more serious problem:- the failure of Christians (who claim to submit to the supreme authority of Jesus Christ, the Word of God, who claimed that He Himself was the very Truth itself), to honour God and accept His Word rather than the wisdom of man. The Bible makes it clear that evolution is false, it states that God created each creature "after its kind" and commanded each creature to reproduce "after its kind". God may have done a certain amount of genetic engineering after the fall, for example, in bringing forth plants with thorns, and animals with carnivorous tendencies — He could even be doing some genetic engineering today — but fortuitous creation and development by naturalistic random chance accidents is utterly opposed to the clear statement "God said ... and it was so". The Bible also makes it clear that creation occurred a fairly short time ago, and all are agreed that without vast ages of time no case whatsoever can be made for evolution.

The fact that many calling themselves Christians accepted evolution and geological time is an illustration of the willingness of many to accept what man says rather than what God says. It is not only in the realm of the pronouncements of science that the "church" has accepted the word of man rather than the Word of God. From the pronouncements of the "Church Fathers" to those of the modern theologians, man's reason has been rated higher than God's word. It is not surprising that the "church" has proved itself a failure — even a disgrace — in many ways.

Every branch of learning is similar in that man uses his own reason to try to come to an understanding of some field of study. The Bible warns (e.g. 1 Corinthians 1 v.20) that the wisdom of man is foolishness. Man's unaided reason is inadequate in any field of study whatsoever. Humanist thinking has succeeded in obscuring this fact, even from many Christians. Throughout society the feeling has sprung up that science represents a sure way to a knowledge of "truth" through man's unaided efforts. That this is not so is painfully obvious, and the scientific community has failed somewhat in its responsibilities to society by not making this widely understood. The admission by Richard Lewontin quoted in the last chapter bears repetition as an illustration of the secular humanist position:-

"We take the side of science in spite of the patent absurdity of some of its constructs, in spite of its failure to fulfil many of its extravagant promises of health and life, in spite of the tolerance of the scientific community for unsubstantiated just-so stories, because we have a prior commitment, a commitment to materialism. It is not that the methods and institutions of science somehow compel us to accept a material explanation of the phenomenal world, but, on the contrary, that we are forced by our a-priori adherence to material causes to create an apparatus of investigation and a set of concepts that produce material explanations, no matter how counterintuitive, no matter how mystifying to the uninitiated. Moreover, that materialism is an absolute, for we cannot allow a Divine Foot in the door."

The secular humanist is so intent on preserving his world view that he cannot allow the possibility of Divine intervention in anything, and must seek a materialistic explanation for everything. But as the outstanding bio-physicist Lee Spetner pointed out "There may not be an adequate naturalistic explanation at all." The secular humanist has closed his mind to that possibility, and considers ignorant or misguided all who have not. Sadly he has also convinced almost everyone else that he really does know what he is talking about.

In order to draw attention to the problem and to point the way towards a solution, a manifesto or "foundational statement" has been devised. It forms the Appendix of this book. It consists of three sections.

The first section sets out a definition of science as being that branch of study which follows the "scientific method". We need to be aware that unless investigations adhere to these precepts they are not scientific. In particular, speculations which propose no genuine means of experimental confirmation are not scientific.

The second section is a historical and philosophical view of the development of modern science, and focuses on the fact that science is essentially a product of the Judeo-Christian world-view. An interesting attestation of this is the fact that some of the groundwork on which modern science was built was done by early Islamic scholars. At that time Islam was effectively a Christian heresy. Mohammed accepted both Old and New Testaments, but added the Koran as a further revelation. Later Islamic theologians gradually altered Islam, rejecting Mohammed's acceptance of the Bible on the grounds (they claimed — without any justification), that it must have been so corrupted since the time of Mohammed that he could not have been talking about the Bible as we know it today. The subsequent contribution of Islamic scholars to scientific advance has been largely conspicuous by its absence.

The third section looks at a code of practice for scientists, and the final section examines the position of the Christian in science. In particular it points out that the Bible is the highest authority in the scientific field, just as it is in every other aspect of life.

In answering the question, then, "what can we do about it", the first step is to recognise that our pride has led us into a number of dead-end streets. Thinking that man's own unaided researches could lead to real truth has led us far from reality in several fields.

The next step must be to publicly admit that fact.

The third step requires that we go back to where we went wrong and start again with a more humble and realistic attitude. An attitude like that shown by the great mathematician and scientist Leonard Euler when he said:- "In our researches into the phenomena of the visible world we are subject to weaknesses and inconsistencies so humiliating that a Revelation was absolutely necessary to us; and we ought to avail ourselves of it with the most powerful veneration".

Appendix

Foundational Statement On Science And Christianity

Introduction

Science is the pursuit of knowledge about the material world around us. It was realised more than four hundred years ago that human reasoning alone is inadequate to ensure accurate conclusions in this field. This realisation led to the development of the "Scientific Method".

The first stage in this method consists of making observations and measurements. Such observations will usually be guided by a preliminary hypothesis or speculation about the way nature may behave.

The second stage consists of studying the patterns suggested by the observations.

The third stage involves proposing hypotheses to explain the observed patterns.

The fourth stage entails predicting the outcome of proposed, but as yet unperformed, experiments on the assumption that a hypothesis describes a general truth.

The fifth stage consists of performing such critical experiments in order to test the predictions made by the hypotheses.

If the predictions are confirmed, then confidence is ascribed to a hypothesis.

If sufficient experimental verification suggests that a hypothesis is universally valid, it is given the status of a scientific theory.

If at any stage experimental results contradict the predictions of a hypothesis or theory it must be modified or abandoned as invalid.

By its nature the scientific method is limited in the range of phenomena which are open to examination. Any field not open to direct experimental testing cannot be considered "scientific". Untestable speculation cannot be considered to be in any way "science". Furthermore, extrapolation far beyond the range of actual experiment, especially into the distant past or the distant future is unscientific.

Although the scientific method has been accepted as the set of guiding rules for scientific investigation for well over two centuries it is clear that in many instances these rules are not being followed. Many scientists appear to be paying lip service to these guiding principles, while pursuing a different course in practice. It has become generally recognised, and clearly documented by such philosophers and historians of science as Kuhn, Polanyi and Popper that personal belief has played a more significant role than experimental observations in several fields of investigation, This has led to the widespread acceptance of "Ad Hoc" theories, unsupported additions to a hypothesis, which explain away instances where predictions are contradicted by observation. In recent years it has led to the general acceptance of the idea of the "Best In The Field" theory. In practice this means the acceptance of a theory which is philosophically acceptable even though contradicted by observation.

It is here proposed that this situation is unsatisfactory. Scientists should address the situation by seriously investigating the experimental evidence for generally accepted theories in order to establish a position in which science can be seen to be based on the highest standards of responsibility and integrity. This is particularly necessary since personal experimental verification by each individual scientist can, of necessity, be only very limited. Knowledge is largely accepted by hearsay and from review of literature.

Historical and Philosophical Perspectives

The scientific method in the form outlined above and nominally accepted today is essentially the product of scientists working under the Judeo-Christian world view. Francis Bacon, widely regarded as the "Father of Modern Science", stressed the value of experiment rather than reason because, he argued, "Nature carries the stamp of the Creator Himself, whereas man's reason carries the stamp of his own foolish pride". Methodical Atheism, the study of Nature on the assumption that God does not exist, has always had its followers, but has always suffered from the inconsistencies of seeking laws without a Law-Giver, absolutes without an Absolute. Since atheism makes man the highest intelligence, the highest authority in the Universe, it has always carried a greater risk of accepting the stamp of the scientist's own foolish pride. The Christian world view was held by most of those involved in modern science, even those not actually professing Christianity, until the latter part of the 19th century. To seek for patterns and order in the creation makes sense within the context of a Creator who works in an orderly fashion. To seek for laws in the creation makes sense within the context of a God who prescribes laws. Absolute values and absolute laws - values and laws which do not depend on agreed convention, but have an inescapable necessity - are possible, and obviously have meaning, in the context of an absolute Creator. It has been said of Newton:- "Were it not for Newton's God, he would never have gone looking for His laws". On the other hand many modern secular humanist scientists have noted that the existence of laws of nature is surprising and inexplicable.

In the latter half of the 19th century scientists in great numbers turned away from the Christian world view, and humanism became the dominant belief system in science. Belief in theories of origins due to random chance materialistic processes became widespread. It became common to entertain unverifiable speculations, unsupported by experimental evidence, to uphold the humanist position that the whole of reality consists solely of deterministic, materialistic processes.

This world view has had drastic effects on almost every aspect of society. Absolute moral standards have no meaning under a purely materialistic, evolutionary world view. If the whole of reality is simply due to random chance processes, then laws and moral values are purely conventional, they can be set by society as a matter of convenience. They can be altered or ignored as a matter of convenience also. This is a marked change from the formerly accepted view that there are absolute standards for moral behaviour and the conduct of life; standards laid down by the Creator of that life.

The consequence for science itself is that science has become entangled in inconsistencies. The humanist world view has proved itself untenable. Examples are legion. Fred Hoyle, after a distinguished career in cosmology, came to the conclusion "the creation of the Universe, like the solution of the Rubik cube, requires an intelligence". George Gaylord Simpson, during a distinguished career in evolutionary biology, had to admit that matter and energy alone were insufficient, and that for the explanation of life "the work required is particular work, it must follow specifications, it requires information on how to proceed". Leif Robinson, holding a prominent position in astronomy, has had to admit that the whole of astronomy is confronted with "ever growing tidal waves of disparate information", evidence which shows that astronomy, like manly other branches of science, is on the wrong track. These scientists came to their conclusions not as a result of abandoning the humanist world view, but simply by admitting that the evidence is overwhelming.

The inconsistencies in present day science have become so severe that there is a growing realisation that materialism is inadequate as a world view. Scientists in great numbers are abandoning pure materialism. Most are taking one of two directions. The first is to return to the Christian position, the acknowledgement of a Creator. The second is to turn to the metaphysical concepts of the religions of the east, particularly Indian ideas centred on a "universal consciousness", a "cosmic force", an "all pervading intelligence". Although very ancient ideas, they are generally being grouped under the title "New Age". Science and civilisation made great advances under the Christian world view predominating in Europe and North America throughout the last few centuries. India, the home of the "New Age" religions, has been remarkably lacking in comparable advance. A new brand of science following "New Age" philosophies is likely to end up with insuperable inconsistencies. The possibility of a universe progressing because of a driving force within itself, because of information developed by and within itself, is contrary to all known experimental evidence, and appears to be as feasible as lifting oneself up by one's own boot straps. The odds seem to be heavily stacked in favour of a world view centred on a Creator. This is not surprising since modern science is essentially a product of this outlook in the first place.

Since science is essentially a product of the Christian world view, and since many scientists are returning to this position, it would be advisable to consider carefully the outlook that should be brought back into this discipline after so many years of absence.

Principles for the Practice Of Science

Science must conform to the principles of the "Scientific Method". This implies that the results of experiment and observation should be taken seriously, even where they conflict with generally accepted or personal theories.

It has been shown repeatedly that a limited number of observations can be fitted into several different hypotheses. Only if all the possible observations relevant to a particular field were known would it be possible to arrive at certainty. Personal commitment to a particular hypothesis based on limited evidence is a very human propensity, but a scientist must be prepared to relinquish any hypothesis which is contradicted by observation.

In all cases where every possible item of information on any field is not available it is necessary to make a priori assumptions. The assumptions form a vital part of any scientific discussion. It should be recognised by all scientists that such assumptions exist, they should be clearly stated as such and not as proven facts, and should remain subject to critical examination.

Science is regarded with considerable respect by the general public, and has great influence on many aspects of society. It is the responsibility of all scientists to report honestly on their work, especially when presenting material to those who are not in a position to appreciate the assumptions involved. The record of scientists in this respect, in recent years, has been alarming. It should be recognised as unacceptable to continue with the currently popular practice of presenting ideas to the public as established, while in reality they are only supported by reasonable probabilities, or which are simply possibilities for which a probability has not even been established. The popular excuse that it would confuse the public to tell them of the uncertainties must be considered dishonest and unacceptable.

Christianity in Science

A scientist approaching science with the Christian world view must obviously follow the scientific method but in addition he recognises a source of information which is of great value in guiding the direction of all research. This source of reference is the Bible, the Word of God, which, by its own testimony, it identifies with the Lord Jesus Christ, as is clearly seen in John 1:1 "In the beginning was the Word, and the Word was with God, and the Word was God". Jesus claimed that this Word is authoritative, as in Matthew 24:35, where He said "Heaven and earth shall pass away, but my words shall not pass away". The Bible testifies that its whole witness is true, as stated in II Timothy 3:16 "All scripture is given by inspiration of God, and is profitable for doctrine, for reproof, for correction, for instruction in righteousness."

A scientist who professes to be a Christian should recognise that the guidance of the Word is not only valuable, but is indispensable. This is seen in Proverbs 3:5-6 "Trust in the LORD with all thine heart; and lean not unto thine own understanding. In all thy ways acknowledge him, and he shall direct thy paths".

Recognition of this has potentially great benefit for scientific investigation, as pointed out in Psalm 119:130 "The entrance of thy words giveth light; it giveth understanding unto the simple", and in Job 32:8 "But there is a spirit in man: and the inspiration of the Almighty giveth them understanding". History suggests that these are no idle promises. God-fearing, Bible-honouring scientists like Newton, Faraday, Euler, Maxwell and Kelvin were responsible for many of the greatest fundamental advances in the whole of science.

If it is valuable to acknowledge the Word of God as a source of understanding, it should be unnecessary to be ashamed of reference to Scripture. As pointed out in Luke 9:26 "For whosoever shall be ashamed of me and of my words, of him shall the Son of man be ashamed, when he shall come in his own glory, and in his Father's, and of the holy angels". Rufus Porter, founder of "Scientific American" more than a century ago, noted in the very first issue:- "First then, let us as rational creatures, be ever ready to acknowledge God .... it is truly surprising that any rational being, who has ever read the inspired writings should willingly forego this privilege, or should be ashamed to be seen engaging in this rational employment, or to have it known that he practices it." Today this very same journal would not consider the acknowledgment of God and the value of the inspired writings of Scripture to be rational employment, and would refuse to publish an article making any such acknowledgment.

A scientist who makes use of the wisdom expressed in the Bible is at an advantage in two important ways. Firstly, any hypothesis which is clearly in direct conflict with Biblical statement can be immediately deduced to be suspect or incorrect, so that undue time need not be spent on attempts at experimental verification. Secondly, positive suggestions for worthwhile lines of investigation may be suggested. Science entails searching for the mode of operation of the creation. Such research is likely to be much more fruitful if it seeks processes compatible with the way the Creator has revealed that He works. The great scientist Johannes Kepler noted that the privilege of a scientist is to think God's thoughts after Him. A researcher is much more likely to arrive at such thoughts if he first studies the general mode of thought that the Creator uses.

A scientist who accepts the authority of the Bible needs to be especially aware of the possibility of error in human reasoning, and the inadequacy of worldly wisdom. He needs to heed the warning in I Corinthians 1:20 "Where is the wise? where is the scribe? where is the disputer of this world? hath not God made foolish the wisdom of this world?" The history of science is full of examples of theories, some of which were held as proven beyond reasonable doubt, which now stand abandoned, an embarrassment to those branches of science which once upheld them, the Phlogiston Theory, Paint-pot Genetics, Caloric, Embryonic Recapitulation …..

Science can deal legitimately only with what can be measured. The Bible deals with what man cannot find out for himself by measurement but can only know by divine revelation. Secular humanistic science has chosen to reject the Bible's revelation and to fit its measurements instead into a set of assumptions consistent with its own worldly wisdom. The resulting anomalies and inconsistencies, the "ever growing tidal waves of disparate information" show this basis to be unsound. The implication is clear. To start with the wisdom of this world and attempt to reconcile conclusions reached on this basis with the wisdom of God is inconsistent. A search for truth must start from a world-view grounded in the Truth.

Bibliography

SCIENCE AT THE CROSS-ROADS, Herbert Dingle, Martin Brian and O'Keeffe, London, 1972

THE BIOTIC MESSAGE Walter J. ReMine, St.Paul Science, ISBN 0-9637999-0-8

CREATION'S TINY MYSTERY, Robert V. Gentry, Earth Science Associates, ISBN 0-9616753-3-0

GEOCENTRICITY, G.D. Bouw, Association for Biblical Astronomy (4527 Wetzel Ave. Cleveland, Ohio 44109, U.S.A.)

DEGENERATIE Peter Schele, Buijten & Schipperheijn, 1997. (The complete translation into English is at http://www.evolution-is-degeneration.com)

UNDERSTANDING THE TIMES, David A. Noebel, Summit Press, Manitou Springs, CO 80829

NOT BY CHANCE Lee Spetner, Judaica Press, New York, 1998

DARWIN'S BLACK BOX, M.J.Behe, Simon and Schuster, 1996.

EVOLUTION: A THEORY IN CRISIS, Michael Denton, Adler and Adler, 1986.

BETRAYERS OF THE TRUTH, William Broad and Nicholas Wade, Touchstone, 1982

THE ORIGIN AND DESTINY OF THE EARTH'S MAGNETIC FIELD. Thomas Barnes. I.C.R. Technical Monograph

VESTIGIAL ORGANS ARE FULLY FUNCTIONAL, J. Bergman and G. Howe, CRS (P.O. Box 28473, Kansas City, MO 64118)

PHYSICS WITHOUT EINSTEIN, Harold Aspden, Sabberton Publications, Southampton, 1969

MODERN AETHER SCIENCE, Harold Aspden, Sabberton Publications, Southampton, 1972

RELATIVITEIT TEGEN HET LIGHT, Luc van Veenhuisen, Uitgeverij Fletio, Amsterdam, 1993

THERMODYNAMICS AND THE DEVELOPMENT OF ORDER, E.L. Williams, CRS

PHYSICS OF THE FUTURE, Thomas Barnes, ICR, 1983.

SEEING RED Halton Arp, Apeiron, Montreal 1998.

SPEAK TO THE EARTH, G.F. Howe, CRS

VARIATION AND FIXITY IN NATURE, F.L. Marsh, CRS

SCIENCE VERSUS EVOLUTION, Malcolm Bowden, Sovereign Publications

APE MEN: FACT OR FALLACY, Malcolm Bowden, Sovereign, Publications

DESIGN AND ORIGINS IN ASTRONOMY, G. Mulfinger, CRS

IN THE MINDS OF MEN, Ian T. Taylor, TFE Publishing Toronto, 1991.

FALSE PROPHETS, Alexander Kohn. Basil Blackwell, New York, 1988

THE EARTH, THE STARS AND THE BIBLE Paul M. Steidl, Baker Book House, Grand Rapids Michigan

IT'S A YOUNG WORLD AFTER ALL, Paul D. Ackerman, Baker Book House, Grand Rapids Michigan

THE AGE OF THE SOLAR SYSTEM, H Slusher. ICR. Tech. Mono.6

THE AGE OF THE EARTH, H Slusher, ICR. Technical Monograph No. 7

THE ORIGIN OF THE UNIVERSE, H Slusher, ICR. Tech. Monograph 8

THE AGE OF THE COSMOS, H Slusher, ICR. Technical Monograph No. 9

WITH EVERY WIND OF DOCTRINE, G.D. Bouw, Tychonian Society, 1984

SCIENTIFIC CREATIONISM H.M. Morris, Creation-Life Publishers, San Diego, California

THE GENESIS FLOOD H.M. Morris and J.C. Whitcomb, Presbyterian and Reformed Publishing Co.

BONE OF CONTENTION, Sylvia Baker, Creation Science Foundation

DE LABORE SOLIS, Walter van der Kamp, Anchor Book and Printing Centre

HOUVAST AAN HET HEMELRUIM, Walter van der Kamp, Uitgevermaatschappij JH. Kok - Kampen, 1985

Periodicals

THE BIBLICAL ASTRONOMER, 4527 Wetzel Avenue, Cleveland, Ohio 44109

CREATION RESEARCH QUARTERLY, I.C.R. El Cajon, CA 92021

GALILEAN ELECTRODYNAMICS, Box 251-A, Boulder, CO 80306

C.E.N. TECHNICAL JOURNAL, C.S.F., POB 302, Sunnybank, Q.4109, Australia

CREATION EX NIHILO, C.S.F., POB 302, Sunnybank, Q.4109, Australia

IMPACT, I.C.R. El Cajon, CA 92021

CREATION, C.S.M. 50, Brecon Ave, Cosham, Portsmouth, PO6 2AW

Ingram Content Group UK Ltd.
Milton Keynes UK
UKHW042002200623
423745UK00001B/63